# Auto Electrics

## Maintenance, fault-finding and repair

Joss Joselyn and Bob Krafft

Newnes Technical Books

**The Butterworth Group**

United Kingdom    **Butterworth & Co (Publishers) Ltd**
London: 88 Kingsway, WC2B 6AB

Australia    **Butterworths Pty Ltd**
Sydney: 586 Pacific Highway, Chatswood, NSW 2067
Also at Melbourne, Brisbane, Adelaide and Perth

Canada    **Butterworth & Co (Canada) Ltd**
Toronto: 2265 Midland Avenue, Scarborough, Ontario M1P 4S1

New Zealand    **Butterworths of New Zealand Ltd**
Wellington: T & W Young Building, 77—85 Customhouse Quay, 1
CPO Box 472

South Africa    **Butterworth & Co (South Africa) (Pty) Ltd**
Durban: 152—154 Gale Street

USA    **Butterworth (Publishers) Inc**
Boston: 10 Tower Office Park, Woburn, Mass. 01801

First published 1980 by Newnes Technical Books,
a Butterworth imprint

© Butterworth & Co (Publishers) Ltd, 1980

**British Library Cataloguing in Publication Data**

Joselyn, Joss
   Auto-electrics.
   1. Automobiles - Electric equipment -
   Maintenance and repair - Amateurs' manuals
   I. Title   II. Krafft, Bob
   629.2'54     TL272     79-40755
   ISBN 0-408-00344-8

Typeset by Butterworths Litho Preparation Department
Printed in England by Page Bros Ltd, Norwich, Norfolk

# Preface

There is no need to be baffled by the complicated electrics in your car. That is the basic message of this book. There are *some* things in automobile electrics that cannot be undertaken by the amateur, but they are very few. With the right sort of knowledge, a few appropriate tools and just a little common sense you can achieve a great deal.

The emphasis throughout is on the practical side of electrical maintenance, fault diagnosis and repair work. With this in mind, the theory has been cut to a minimum and practical repair information substituted. The theoretical explanations that are included are much simplified, and to the purist and anyone who really grasps the theoretical side they will seem something less than exact. However, this approach simplifies things for the beginner and has no effect at all on the accuracy of the remainder of the book. Expert and beginner alike will benefit from the practical trouble-shooting and repair aspects.

Much of the information is based on the Lucas system and equipment used in British cars. Foreign electrics, however, are very similar and what differences there are involve detail only.

Tools required have been kept to a minimum. For most testing jobs a small bulb holder with two leads, fitted with small crocodile clips, will be used. Add to these a couple of lengths of wire about one metre (three feet) long, again with clips at each end.

You will need a set of spanners to fit the nuts and bolts on your particular car, plus a couple of small BA sizes; large, medium and small screwdrivers to cope with both slotted and cross-headed screws; a hammer; two pairs of pliers, one with long narrow tips (needle-nose); and a pair of wire cutters. Almost all the work detailed throughout the book can be accomplished with just these tools.

The fact that the average car owner who tackles his own repair work is not a wealthy man has not been forgotten. The accent throughout is also on saving money.

# Contents

# 1 Wiring

Like the veins and arteries in the human body or the domestic plumbing system in a house, the wiring loom in the car is essentially a distribution network. Car wiring is not something that the majority of drivers take a great interest in — until something goes wrong. Then, after a baffled look at the bunches of multicoloured spaghetti in the car, they resort to the circuit in the car handbook or workshop manual. This resembles a map of Hampton Court Maze, smothered in unintelligible symbols — and at this point, they give up and telephone the auto-electrician.

There's no need. It can be explained quite simply. All the colours in the wiring loom mean something and are colour coded to indicate not only which individual circuit they are part of but in which part of that circuit they are situated.

The wiring circuit becomes a lot simpler to understand as soon as you realise that it is not just one circuit but several, and that although they are linked together it's not difficult to separate them if you wish.

All those separate circuits are based on a single archetypal basic circuit. This consists of a source of supply (battery), a device for breaking and completing the circuit (switch), a working unit (bulb, motor or whatever), and the necessary wiring. See Figure 1.1.

While the switch is open, no current can flow in the circuit. As soon as the switch is closed, current flows from the battery, through the wiring to the switch, across the closed contacts and on to the consumer unit, through the unit (which will light up if it is a bulb, or, if a motor, will turn and perform whatever its function is in the car) and then back to the battery to complete the circuit.

Invariably the car body/chassis unit is used as the earth-return side of the circuit. One terminal of the battery is connected to this by means of a braided metal strap, and the bulb, motor or other consumer unit is also connected to the car body (earth). Once the switch is closed, the consumer unit will continue to operate either until the switch is opened to interrupt the flow or until the energy stored in the battery is used up.

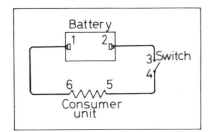

**Figure 1.1** Basic circuit, consisting of battery, switch, working unit and necessary wiring

**FAULT-FINDING PRINCIPLES**

Let us consider the faults that can occur in this simple circuit, because these will be exactly the same faults that will be experienced in the more involved circuits in the car. As an example, take the case of a lamp circuit.

When we close the switch, we expect the lamp to light. If it doesn't, the fault can be in one or more parts of the circuit and we shall need to check the battery, the switch, the lamp itself and the wiring.

This is where the first simple piece of equipment is required. If you are already so equipped, you may like to use a voltmeter, but in most cases it is best to use a test lamp.

It is possible to buy a test lamp quite cheaply at any car accessory shop. In appearance it is like a small electrical screwdriver, with a steel probe instead of the blade and incorporating a small bulb inside the transparent plastic handle. From the handle end runs a length of wire, with a crocodile clip fitted to the end.

A home-made substitute is just as good. You will need a bulb of suitable voltage rating to match the battery (which could be 6 volts, but nowadays will almost certainly be 12 volts). It is best, in practice, to use a 21-watt bulb: this is big enough to show up bad or high-resistance connections, is not too high for sensitive circuits, and, if necessary, gives enough light to use as an inspection or lead light.

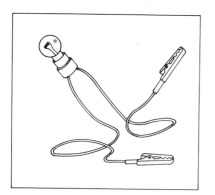

**Figure 1.2** Home-made circuit tester

The bulb is then fitted into a bulb holder — one removed from an old side lamp or flasher lamp is suitable — and two wires about one metre (three feet) long are connected to the terminals. A small crocodile clip is fitted to the loose end of each lead, and a prod, made of a 10 cm (4 in) length of stiff brass wire, is held in one of the crocodile clips. As its name implies, this is used for prodding various points in the circuit when testing. The home-made tester is shown in Figure 1.2.

It is usual, of course, to prod first at anything that looks suspicious, but eventually it comes down to a systematic check, using the following sequence.

• With one test lead clipped to the battery terminal (marked 1 in Figure 1.1) and the test prod pressed against the other battery terminal (2), the lamp should light. This is just a preliminary check to ensure that the battery does have a charge in it. If the lamp doesn't light, either the battery is discharged (flat) or the test lamp or the connections to it are faulty.
• Check the bulb tester on another battery and then, if it lights this time, carry out the first test again.
• If the first test is satisfactory, leave the lead connected to the battery terminal (1) and press the probe on to the switch terminal at (3). If the light comes on, the circuit between points 2 and 3 is sound.
• Close the switch and test at point 4. A satisfactory result proves the switch is in order. Repeat at point 5, the consumer unit terminal, to check the circuit at this point.

● A failure of the test lamp to light at any point denotes a failure of the circuit between that point and the previous point where a positive result was obtained.
● If we now test between battery terminal (1) and point 6, the bulb will obviously not light because both these points are at the same potential and there will be no current flow. To test this section, therefore, the crocodile clip will have to be transferred to the other battery terminal (2). The bulb should now light between points 2 and 6, thus proving the final section of the circuit.
● If the circuit passes every test in the above sequence, but the consumer unit (bulb, motor, etc.) still does not work when switched on, the consumer unit itself must be faulty.

This method is the basis of all test procedures, although there are variations and other methods that are detailed later in the book. There are also a number of time-saving short cuts, which will be described as they arise.

## COMBINED CIRCUITS

Obviously all the circuits in the car are not as uncomplicated as the one just mentioned, although the same principle applies to all of them. If exactly that circuit were used for every bulb, every motor and every electrical item in the car, each circuit would be very simple but the sheer bulk of wiring and the duplication of switches etc. would make the system as a whole very complicated indeed. For this reason some circuits are combined; this means that, although the circuitry becomes more involved, the overall system is simplified.

Let's take an actual example: side and rear lights. Figure 1.3 shows what the simple circuit evolves into. Instead of each circuit having its own switch, there is now only one — which is all that's necessary, since all the lamps need to be switched on and off at the same time. Also eliminated are all

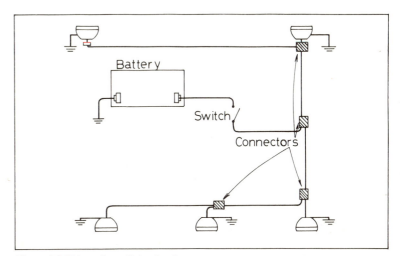

Figure 1.3 Side and rear light circuit

the return wires to the earth side of the battery. Instead of these, all the components (lamps in this case) are earthed, and so is the second battery terminal. The triangular symbol is one of two international symbols denoting earth. Earthing is achieved normally by the metal casing of the lamp being bolted firmly to the metal chassis of the car, the earth terminal of the battery being similarly connected by means of a braided earth strap, as already described.

There has been another change to arrive at the Figure 1.3 circuit. In order to economise still further on cable, and additionally simplify the wiring harness or loom, the wiring after the switch has been reduced to a single cable; this is linked to the various lamps by means of cable connectors, only one wire going forward to the front lamps, for instance, and only one to the rear. These connectors are also known as 'snap' connectors and are used in conjunction with 'bullet' terminals.

As a second example, consider the headlamp circuit. Basically similar to the side-light circuit, it is a little more complicated as it requires two switches, one to turn the lights on and off and the other to switch the headlamp beams from

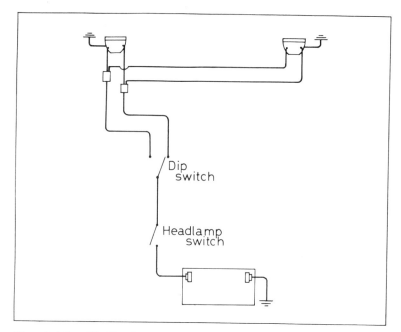

**Figure 1.4** Simplified headlamp circuit

main to dipped beam. Each headlamp, of course, is virtually two lights — either separate bulbs or just separate filaments. Again, using connectors to simplify the layout, the circuit is shown in Figure 1.4.

Note that throughout these combined circuits the original basic circuit for each lamp can still be traced out quite simply and can be tested in the same way, with the test-lamp leads connected at the appropriate points. When making tests at some distance from the battery, remember that the clip does not necessarily have to be connected to battery terminal 1. As this is connected to the chassis or body of the vehicle, it is quite sufficient to anchor one crocodile clip to any convenient point on the bodywork of the car. Make sure, however, that you get a good 'electrical' connection to the metal and do not clamp on to metal insulated by paint or by rust. Bright or plated parts are usually best.

When using the test lamp, always check the lamp across the battery before commencing any tests. Check it at intervals during the testing, and check it again after testing to ensure that it is still working. It can be infuriating to carry out a series of tests on an involved circuit, only to find that the test lamp itself failed at some point during the procedure and that all the work has to be done over again.

## IDENTIFYING WIRING IN THE CAR

In the wiring loom in the car, all the cables travelling along a similar route are bound together with some form of tape or passed through a sleeve in such a way that they support each other and the loom gains some mechanical strength. When the loom is laid out in the car, the cable ends emerge from the harness binding in the right place, are the right length, and are equipped with the necessary terminal ends to enable them to be joined to the various components for which they are intended.

To the inexperienced, the made-up loom looks like an electrical nightmare. Moreover it appears to bear no resemblance whatever to the wiring diagram that is printed in the owner's handbook or maintenance manual. This is because the printed version is often drawn as a theoretical circuit and reduced in size to fit in the handbook, making the lines thin and too close together to follow. Better are the physical circuit in Figure 1.5 and the type of theoretical diagram in Figure 1.6. In the former, the actual units are shown in their positions in the car but it is difficult to trace a given wire through the diagrammatic harness. The theoretical diagram in Figure 1.6 is clearer to follow but confusion is reintroduced because the layout of the unit symbols in no way matches their location in the car.

The Lucas system is used on the majority of cars built in Britain. Some cars, such as Fords built elsewhere in Europe, use a Continental colour code for their wiring. There are also Japanese, French, German and Italian systems, which are different again. The table on page 134 shows various alternatives to the Lucas code.

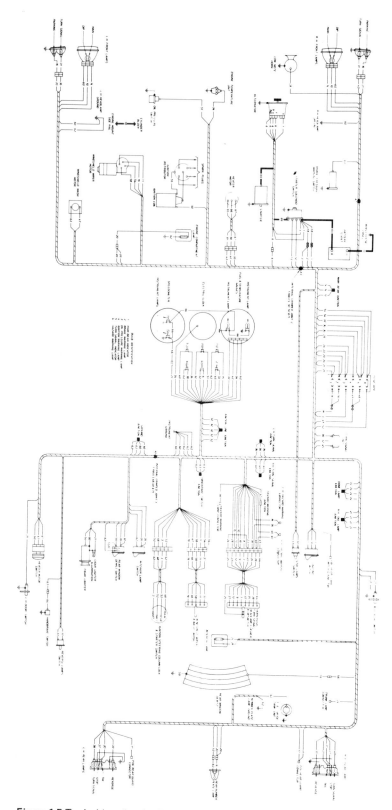

**Figure 1.5** Typical handbook wiring diagram: 'physical' (Chevette, courtesy Vauxhall Motors Ltd)

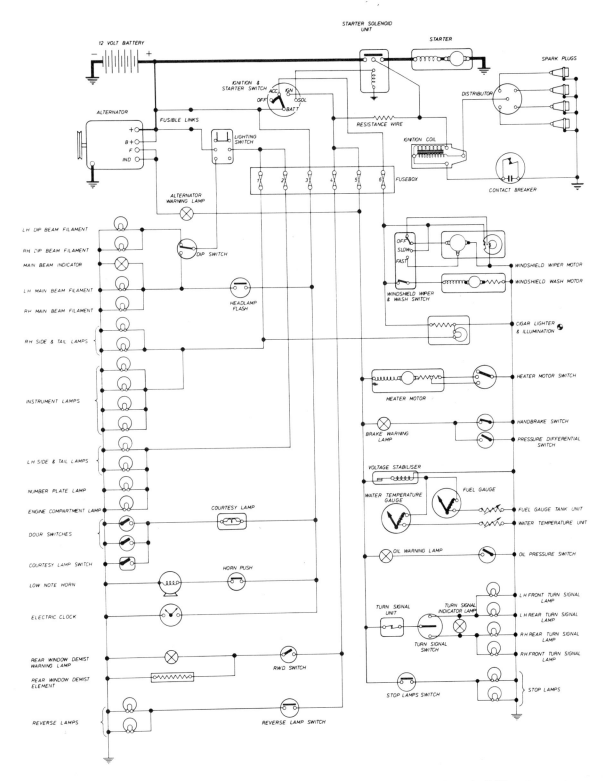

**Figure 1.6** Typical handbook wiring diagram: 'theoretical' (Chevette, courtesy Vauxhall Motors Ltd)

The Lucas colour coding system is quite straightforward and, to some extent, logical. It is based on seven colours: brown, white, red, blue, green, purple and black. *Black* wires are all earth connections. Other single-colour wires are used for 'live' wires to and from switches.

There is a second series of wires that have a main or 'base' colour with a second colour superimposed in the form of a thin trace line. These cables are used between switches and consumer units, etc.

The different base colours are used to denote various sections of the vehicle wiring. Thus all the main feed wires from the battery to switches, etc. are *brown*, as are cables in the charging circuit. Wiring in the ignition circuit is *white*, with coloured traces to denote certain sections.

Side and rear light wiring has *red* as the base colour, while headlamp wiring is *blue*. The latter acquires a white trace for main-beam wiring and a red trace for dipped-beam wires.

Auxiliary units that are controlled by the ignition switch (i.e. they switch off automatically when the ignition is turned off and cannot be switched on without switching on the ignition first) have *green* as the basic colour. Direction indicators and windscreen wipers come into this group. Auxiliary units not controlled by the ignition switch have *purple* as the base colour of their cables. Into this group come courtesy lights and often the horn.

Later cars, with more accessories and therefore more wiring, sometimes have three extra wiring colours: *light green, slate* and *pink*. Cars with overdrive fitted (or some of them, anyway) have an extra colour to denote the overdrive wiring: *yellow*.

The circuit or wiring diagram in a typical owner's handbook or workshop manual is usually reproduced only in black and white. Wiring colours, however, are shown by letters with an accompanying key. Where the cable concerned is a base colour with a secondary (trace) colour, the main colour is indicated first, followed by the trace colour.

The usual code for wiring colours on a black and white circuit diagram is as follows:

| B | Black | N | Brown | U | Blue |
|---|---|---|---|---|---|
| G | Green | P | Purple | W | White |
| K | Pink | R | Red | Y | Yellow |
| LG | Light green | S | Slate | | |

**Main feed and charging-circuit wiring**

If we take an average car wiring diagram and check the wiring colour system from the main source of supply (the battery), we will find that one battery terminal is connected to the chassis or car body via a short, heavy cable. This may be fairly rigid insulated cable, a woven wire strap or a round plaited wire cable. Known as the earth strap or earth cable, it is very important — every circuit in the car uses this cable as its return connection to the battery.

From the other battery terminal runs another heavily insulated cable, which connects the battery to the starter solenoid switch. This may be mounted on the car body, on the engine or on the starter motor itself.

From one end (or in a few cases, from both ends) of this cable, one or more fairly thick brown cables are taken to various switches, junction boxes, etc. It's not possible to give an exact description here — this is where the differences between one car's circuit and another start. There's no alternative to working out the circuit on your own car by looking at the actual wiring and comparing it with the circuit in the handbook.

If you've got an ammeter fitted, there will be a thick brown wire that runs to this, and possibly a thinner one of the same colour that goes to a fusebox to supply the horn and courtesy light. From the second ammeter terminal, a brown wire with a white trace will go to the control box (if one is fitted). In a car that has an alternator rather than a dynamo, one brown/white wire will go to the main alternator terminal and another brown/white wire will go to the ignition switch, with a branch to the lighting switch. The wire has changed from plain brown to brown-and-white to indicate that something has happened in the circuit; in this case, it has passed through the ammeter.

If a control box and dynamo are fitted, there will be a brown/white wire from ammeter to control box and a brown/blue wire to the lighting and ignition switches. Again the change in trace colour denotes another unit in the circuit.

There will also be three more brown wires: one of heavy gauge with a yellow trace, running from the control box to the generator main terminal, a thin brown/yellow one to the instrument panel for the ignition warning light, and a thin brown/green wire to the generator field terminal. These connections will be explained more fully in Chapters 4 and 5.

You can now see that the whole of the wiring of the feed and charging system consists of a few cables, all of a basic brown colour but with different coloured traces.

**Ignition wiring**

Wires lead out from the ignition switch, all with the base colour white. A white/red cable connects to the solenoid (closing the solenoid operates the starter). There's a plain white wire that links into the fuse box to provide current for the ignition-controlled accessories, and then goes on to the coil to provide ignition low-tension (l.t.) current. Another white wire goes to the ignition warning light.

**Lighting wiring**

Current is fed into the lighting switch via a plain brown wire (or brown with a colour trace, depending on the type of main feed circuit). Leading out will be one or more red wires to the side lights, rear lights and number-plate light. There will also be a red cable connecting to the panel-light switch, and this is linked in turn to the various panel lights via a red/white cable.

If the side lights are fused, the red wire from the switch will go to the fuse, and red wires with a green or blue trace (to show they are fused) go to the lamps.

From a third terminal on the lighting switch, a blue wire (the headlamp circuit is basically blue) goes to feed the dipswitch. From here blue/white and blue/red wires — the trace denotes the second switching — lead to the headlamp main-beam and dipped-beam circuits respectively.

## Auxiliary-unit wiring

From the fusebox numerous plain green wires lead out to the various ignition-controlled accessories. One goes to the flasher unit, and from here a light-green/brown wire links to the direction-indicator switch, from which green/white and green/red cables lead to the direction-indicator lamps themselves.

Another plain green wire links from the fusebox to the stop-lamp switch, and this connects to the stop lamps via a green/purple wire. Fuel gauge, screen wipers, etc. all use a similar system: plain green wires in, and green with a trace out.

Auxiliaries that are not controlled by the ignition switch are also protected by a fuse. The feed wires from fusebox to courtesy lights and horn are plain purple. From courtesy lamp to switch the wire is purple/white, and from horn to switch, purple/black.

There are plenty of other wires not mentioned, but the way the circuit is built up can be seen from the foregoing. Remember that your car may be wired on some system other than the Lucas one described here. Always check with the coded circuit in your handbook.

## MAINTENANCE AND REPAIR

Maintaining the wiring loom is hardly a chore. There is, in fact, very little that can be done to it until something goes wrong, and then it's more a fault-finding exercise than maintenance.

Two things are important, however. First, keep an eye on all the fixing clips for the wiring harness. Ensure that, if the harness is removed at any time, it is always firmly replaced in its fixing clips. Second, check occasionally to ensure that the grommets that protect wires passing through metal bulkheads are in place. If they are missing, the insulation around the cables can chafe on the sharp metal; this can result in fuse-blowing problems at best and a wiring fire at worst.

What do you do after a fire? The actual burning is usually stopped by switching off the ignition, but to be safe follow this by disconnecting the battery. Finding the trouble will be a matter of checking what components have stopped working, and then using the test-lamp routine described at the beginning of this chapter. Once the source of the trouble is found (and it will almost certainly be one or more burnt wires), a decision can be made on what to do about it.

If there is one burnt wire, this will make discovery of the original trouble simple. If a bunch of them is burnt, it could be more difficult. Generally damaged insulation will be the problem, perhaps because wires were clamped under something during repairs or because chafing occurred as a result of a missing grommet. Once the cause of the burn-out has been discovered and put right, a start can be made on repairing the damage.

Begin by detaching the damaged part of the loom from the car. Often nowadays the loom is made in several parts, joined by multi-pin plugs. This makes it considerably easier to detach just one section. Depending on where the damage is, it may be easier to cut away part of the loom and then rebuild just the burnt bit.

Cut away the loom wrapping with a sharp knife, and part the wires to ensure a thorough inspection for damage. If there are several wires of the same colour, or if there is any chance of confusion, mark the ends. Use electrician's pliers or side cutters to cut out the wiring that is damaged. Strip back the insulation at the ends and join in new lengths of wire, the same gauge and colour as the existing cables. Twist the ends together and lightly coat them with solder so that they don't come apart again (see Figure 1.7). Don't overdo this, however, or else the joints will become too bulky. (Another idea is to stagger the individual joints to avoid bulkiness.) Tape each joint carefully with proper insulation tape and then, finally, wind tape spirally around the whole area of the repair and put the loom back into the car. It's a good idea to use the test lamp to check the continuity of each cable before re-installing the loom, just to ensure that no mistakes have been made.

Further information on techniques with cables is given in Chapter 10.

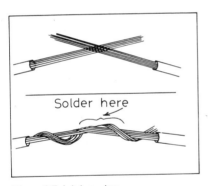

**Figure 1.7** Joining wires

# 2 Battery

The history of electricity started with the *simple cell*. This consisted of a piece of copper sheet and a piece of zinc sheet suspended in a dilute solution of sulphuric acid. When the two plates were joined together with a piece of wire, a small current flowed through the circuit.

Since it was not known just what was happening, it was assumed (wrongly) that the current was flowing from the copper plate to the zinc plate, and these were labelled positive and negative respectively.

This original simple cell was improved by various people, and the Clarke cell, Leclanché cell, di-chromate cell and many others were produced. They all had the same failing: when the chemicals were used up the cell was useless as it could not be recharged.

Today, although some types of simple cell are still used experimentally, only one — the Leclanché cell — is used commercially. This is the familiar dry battery used in torches, radios, etc.

## LEAD—ACID CELL

Development of the simple cell eventually resulted in the *secondary cell*. The most common form of this is the lead—acid cell, still the basis of the modern car battery.

Each cell of this type consists of a positive plate formed of an oxide of lead and a negative plate formed of a spongy form of lead, both suspended in a weak sulphuric-acid *electrolyte*. When the plates are connected by a wire, a chemical action occurs inside the battery and a current flows through the circuit.

The two plates slowly turn to lead sulphate and the acid turns to water. After a while, the action comes to an end. If, however, the current flow through the cell can be reversed, the action inside the battery is also reversed; the plates become lead oxide again, and the electrolyte becomes sulphuric acid. The cell is then in a condition to give another supply of current.

This is, of course, a very simple explanation of the rather complicated process that goes on inside the cell, but it is sufficient to understand how the cell is charged and discharged.

A crude cell like this would give only a small current, and that for only a short time. A practical and usable current can

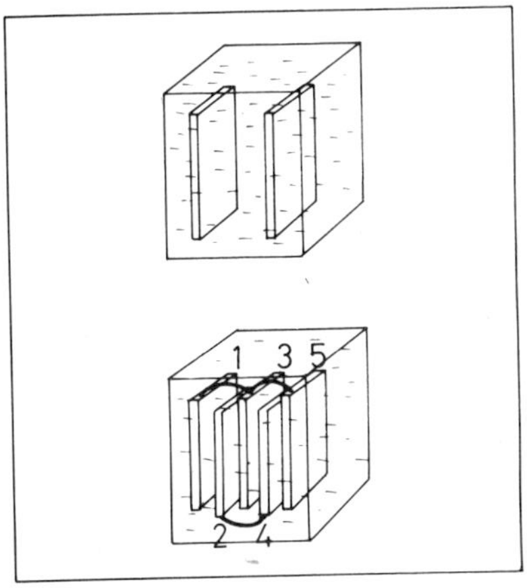

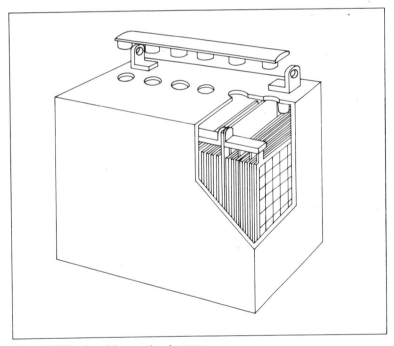

**Figure 2.1** Basic cell and its development

be obtained by means of a more complicated arrangement, however. Instead of just two plates, positive and negative, the modern battery has inside it interleaved groups of plates (Figure 2.1). These are joined alternately: 1, 3, 5, 7 and 2, 4, 6, 8 etc., with a negative plate at each end. The amount of current that can be drawn from a cell depends on the surface area of the plates; i.e. the more and bigger the plates, the more powerful the cell will be.

In practice the cell contains seven or more plates of about 200 square centimetres (30 square inches) per side. The interlocked plates are further interleaved with sheets of wood or plastic called separators, which allow a very compact assembly. Figure 2.2 shows the inside of a modern battery.

Each cell will develop a voltage or electrical 'pressure' of around two volts, so usually six cells are joined together inside one unit to form a battery capable of providing 12 volts. There are a few cars still around with 6-volt batteries, but these are very much the exception.

**Figure 2.2** What's inside a modern battery

All the time the battery was being developed, the basic assumption that current flows from positive to negative persisted. Not until the introduction of thermionic valves in radio and similar equipment was it realised that the flow is really from negative to positive. By this time is was too late to do anything about the nomenclature. All the published textbooks already contained the wrong information, and it would have cost a fortune to change existing batteries, switchboards and electrical equipment, already wrongly marked.

Fortunately, for general use the direct current (d.c.) system was already being superseded by alternating current (a.c.), and this really only left the motor industry as a large user of direct-current installation.

Incidentally, no matter what you're told elsewhere, it doesn't make the slightest difference to the operation of *most* electrical equipment whether the system has positive or negative earth. However, some specialised equipment (such as radios, cassette players etc.) may be designed for a specific polarity, and the majority of alternators on later cars are designed for negative earth working, purely for economic and design reasons. It is cheaper to make a negative-earth alternator than a positive-earth one.

If a unit *has* been designed for a specific polarity, great care must always be taken to connect it the right way round. If the connections are reversed and the unit switched on, serious damage will be done to the transistors in the circuit.

## MAINTENANCE

Not a great deal of battery maintenance is required. Generally it is enough to keep it clean and topped up with distilled water, and to ensure that the terminal connections are clean and tight.

Keeping it clean consists merely of wiping the top with a piece of rag before and after topping up. Before, to get rid of any dirt; after, to mop up any spillage of distilled or de-ionised water.

Do not use anything else for topping up — certainly never ordinary tap water. It is best to use one of the special dispensers sold for the purpose, so that topping up can be done a little at a time, under control and not splashing water everywhere and overfilling. The latter should always definitely be avoided.

Keep the electrolyte level just above the top of the *plates*, not the separators. (The bits you can see at the sides when you look through the holes in the cell lids are the tops of the wood or plastic separators.) It is sufficient to add water until you just get an unbroken surface: if you add more, the cell is overfilled. When the battery is charged and the interior gets warm, the electrolyte expands; with overfilling, some of the electrolyte may be forced up through the vents in the lids, resulting in loss of electrolyte and a nasty mess of corroded metal around the battery.

You will probably find that monthly checks of the electrolyte level are sufficient in the winter, but when the warmer weather comes the evaporation rate will be increased and

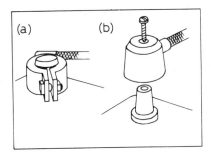

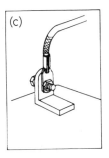

**Figure 2.3** Three types of battery cable connection: (a) clamp, (b) inverted cup, (c) Ford type

topping up will have to be tackled at weekly intervals. Undue water loss, however, should not be tolerated. This could well be due to overcharging; see chapters 4 and 5.

The other basic maintenance job is to care for the battery terminals. There are three kinds. One is a heavy metal clamp that fits round the terminal post and is pinched tight by a nut and bolt. Another is the inverted cup type, made from a lead alloy and secured by a self-tapping screw. Finally there is the Ford type, which uses a flat plate on the battery (instead of the more usual round post) and a flat plate on the battery cables; both plates are drilled and a nut and bolt are used to clamp them together. See Figure 2.3.

Cleanliness and good electrical contact are essential with all three types. This means cleaning both terminal posts and the cable connectors. Round terminal posts are best tackled using a strip of glass paper. Use a reciprocating action to bring them up to bright metal, but they do not need to be smooth and polished. Avoid taking off too much metal if you can, or eventually the clamp terminals may not fit tightly enough on the tapered posts. Use a coarse round file to clean up the metal inside the clamp-type and cup-type connectors; a flat file will cope with the Ford type. Before refixing all three types, coat the mating surfaces with a smear of petroleum jelly. This will help stop sulphation (seen as a dense white powder) and make the connectors easily removable when required.

If, with the cup-type connector, the hole in the post has lost its thread, try melting some lead into it and then recutting the thread with a new self-tapping screw.

If the cup-type terminal fits too loosely on the terminal post, don't try packing it out with silver paper; a better idea is to hold the cup terminal in your hand and tap the side of it with a hammer until the inside closes up a little and the cup is a tight fit once more.

If the terminals have been allowed to deteriorate to such an extent that they have collected growths of a powdery white and green oxide, they will have to be cleaned using hot water and domestic soda. Remember too to check the other end of both leads to ensure that they are making sound contact. If the earth lead is dirty or corroded where it bolts to the chassis or body, take it off and clean it, coat with petroleum jelly and replace. Treat the other end of the 'live' lead where it bolts to the solenoid in the same way.

## TESTING AND CHARGING

To test the battery, a *hydrometer* is used. This consists of a glass tube with a nozzle at the lower end and a bulb at the top. Inside the tube is a weighted float with graduations marked on the stem. When electrolyte is drawn up into the

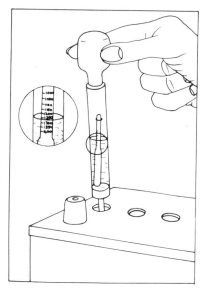

**Figure 2.4** Hydrometer for testing specific gravity

tube the float will settle at a certain level, depending on the strength or 'specific gravity' of the electrolyte, i.e. the proportion of acid to water. See Figure 2.4.

Earlier in this chapter it was mentioned that, as the battery is discharged, some of the acid turns to water, then as the battery is charged the water is changed back to acid. If the hydrometer gives a low reading, the battery is in a discharged condition; if the reading is high, the battery is charged.

Normally a charged battery gives a reading of about 1.250–1.290. Half charged it should read between about 1.190 and 1.210, and if it's discharged the reading will be between 1.110 and 1.150 on the hydrometer scale. Readings will also vary according to the temperature, but those given are accurate when the temperature is between 13 and 18 °C (55–65 °F).

You can buy a basic hydrometer from any motor accessory shop, and it is extremely simple to use. Measurements are conducted on each cell in turn. Use the rubber bulb to draw enough electrolyte into the glass tube to enable the float inside to float freely. On the float is printed a scale, and it's a matter of noting down the reading where the float is cut by the surface of the electrolyte. Compare all the figures afterwards. They should be approximately the same: a large variation between cells probably means buying a new battery, because the low-reading cells have failed.

Never measure the specific gravity immediately after topping up the battery. Either take the car for a run, use a battery charger for an hour, or leave the battery alone for a few hours. The idea is to allow the electrolyte to mix thoroughly.

If the battery in question is a spare or is on a car that is seldom used, it will need charging periodically. To prevent the battery from deteriorating, keep its specific gravity above 1.150, i.e. more than 25% charged.

If the battery is in a discharged or partially discharged condition, it can be brought back up to strength by using the charging system in the car (taking it out for a drive) or by connecting up to some form of battery charger. There are many different types of these, ranging from large commercial types, used by garages etc., down to small home chargers. Ideally these should have an output of up to five amps.

Before connecting up the battery charger, check whether the car is fitted with an alternator. If it is, it's best to play safe and disconnect the battery from the car. The alternator's diode pack may be damaged if it's left connected.

Loosen the battery's filler caps so that gas can escape. Clip the battery charger's red lead to the positive terminal of the battery, turning the clip hard on the post to ensure the crocodile teeth bite and secure good electrical contact.

Connect the black lead in the same way to the negative terminal. Find a good steady position for the charger and then plug in to the mains and switch on.

When the charger is connected to a discharged battery, the output shown on the meter will be somewhere towards maximum; as the battery becomes charged, the rate will drop off until the fully charged condition is reached. The reading will then be probably one or two amps. To charge up a totally 'flat' battery will probably take about 12 hours, but it is a good idea to check towards the end of this period with a hydrometer. The battery is fully charged when readings between 1.250 and 1.290 are recorded.

During the latter stages of charging each cell of the battery will be bubbling and gassing. This occurs when the chemical change in the battery is completed. Any further passage of current starts to split the water component of the electrolyte into hydrogen and oxygen, which are given off as a gas.

The mixture of gases given off is highly explosive and any naked light or even a cigarette brought near to the battery can cause an explosion, which can split the battery wide open. Switch the charger off at the mains before disconnecting from the battery — a spark from a terminal might trigger an explosion.

If one or more cells are gassing more violently than the others, this is often a sign that the battery is faulty. If, when the battery is reconnected to the car, there is insufficient power to turn the engine, take the filler caps off the battery and look into the cells while the starter is operated. If one or more cells then start to bubble violently, this also is a sign of a faulty battery.

The only other way a battery can be abused is by not holding it in position properly or by overtightening the holding clamps. If it's free to shift about, the casing could be cracked and the terminals could be loosened; internal plate damage could also result. Overtightening the typical angle clamp used to hold a battery can also cause case damage, cracks and leakage of the electrolyte. Damage can also ensue from over-enthusiastic tightening and untightening of the terminal clamps. The most likely place for leaks to occur is around the terminal posts or around the top of the battery case, just under the lid. A sign of leakage is the formation of white crystals and deposits.

Depending on where the crack is, it doesn't necessarily mean the end of the battery. There are battery sealers on the market that will repair the kind of crack mentioned above, or sometimes the job can be done by melting sealing wax into the crack. Cracks below the level of the electrolyte, however, cannot really be satisfactorily repaired (although we have heard of people making a temporary seal by running a hot soldering iron along the crack).

## BATTERY BUYING

When buying a new battery, you can usually get the right type merely by specifying the car to the retailer. It can, however, pay to think a little before rushing out and buying the first one on the shelf. There is quite a large difference between the top-quality battery and the cheap and cheerful replacement. Unfortunately there is no certain way of telling what you're buying. The number of plates per cell is sometimes quoted as a good guide. Certainly a nine-plate battery is designed as a heavier duty unit than a seven-plate one, but quality really depends more on the thickness of the lead coating on the plates: a difference of 0.25 mm (0.01 in) in the thickness can have a considerable effect on battery performance.

What undoubtedly is important is to buy a battery with the correct ampere-hour rating. This is a measure of capacity. The idea is that a 48 A h battery when fully charged will deliver a current of 1 amp for 48 hours, or 3 amps for 16 hours, or 12 amps for 4 hours, etc. It is sometimes a good idea to buy the heavy-duty version of the battery you require. This usually has the same physical dimensions but a higher ampere-hour rating. It will, of course, cost more but could be a worthwhile buy.

The only other safeguards are the battery name and the guarantee. If you buy a very well-known make of battery you'll get a good guarantee with it, probably for two years, but it will cost more. The very much cheaper battery might still be a good buy, particularly if you're not planning to keep the car for long.

Of course, a very important thing to consider before you buy is: are you _sure_ you need a new battery? Could it not be some fault in the charging system? Maybe it's just a slipping fanbelt! One good way to find out is to have the battery checked by a garage or an auto-electrician who has the proper equipment, including a cell tester, to find out. So many owners make the mistake of walking into a garage and asking them to fit a new battery. The garageman won't argue. He'll fit it whether it's necessary or not.

If the battery is beginning to fail, it's most likely to become evident with the first cold weather in autumn. Current regeneration falls off as the temperature drops, and in freezing conditions it can be 40% down on its summer performance. Remember also that engine oil thickens in cold weather, so the engine is harder to turn over anyway. The inevitable result, every year, is a large number of batteries that suddenly can't cope with starting — always the hardest job the battery has to do.

Keep your battery clean and topped up with electrolyte, check it occasionally and keep it charged, and it should outlast its guarantee.

# 3 Starter motor

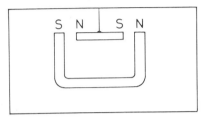

**Figure 3.1** Magnets are pole-seeking when free to move

An important fact about a magnet is that it is 'pole seeking'. When free to move, one end of a bar magnet will want to point north and is called its north pole; the other end will want to point south and is known as its south pole. However, more important for an electric motor is that, with magnets, *like poles repel, unlike poles attract*. A simple experiment to prove this point is to suspend a small bar magnet between the jaws of a horseshoe magnet. The bar magnet will swing to line up with its north pole pointing to the horseshoe's south pole, and vice versa (Figure 3.1).

## BASIC ELECTRIC MOTOR

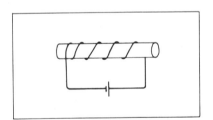

**Figure 3.2** Basic electromagnet

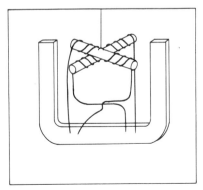

**Figure 3.3** Rotating magnets in one direction only

If you would like to continue to experiment, you can find out exactly how an electric motor works — which is of great practical value when checking for faults. If, however, you would rather skip the next bit you will not be missing any practical information on fault finding and repairs.

For the next stage in the experiment, take a short iron bar that is non-magnetic and wind a few turns of wire round it. Connect the free ends of the wire to a battery (a torch battery will do) and you have a magnet — in fact an *electromagnet* (Figure 3.2). Suspend this between the jaws of your horseshoe magnet, and the bar will line up north to south and south to north.

Now, here is the most important part. Reverse the battery connections and the 'polarity' will also reverse. The bar will swing round into an exactly opposite position, but it may swing clockwise or anti-clockwise.

To ensure that it always swings in the same direction, take another small bar, form a cross with the first piece, and wind the same number of turns of wire on each (Figure 3.3). You will now have four loose ends of wire, which you must mark for easy identification. Suspend the cross between the poles of the horseshoe magnet and connect one of the coils to the battery. The cross will swing round and one bar will line up with the horseshoe poles. Disconnect this pair of wires and connect the second pair: this will make the second bar swing to line up. Now go back to the first pair and reconnect them — *but in reverse* — and the cross will swing again *in the same direction*. If you could keep swopping the pairs of wires you

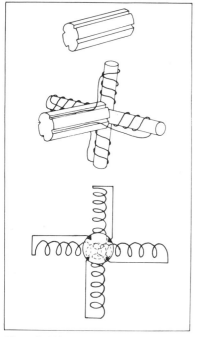

**Figure 3.4** Home-made electric motor

would have continuous rotation, but your wires would become well and truly twisted.

Now we come to the final stage in the experiment. Take the cork of a wine bottle and score four shallow grooves in it at twelve, three, six, and nine o'clock, the whole length of the cork. Stick one end of the cork to the centre of the cross, bare the ends of the coil wires and lay them into the grooves alternately, cutting them to length. Cut four narrow strips of foil the same length as the cork and lay them over the wires, taking care that the edges do not touch each other. Bind them securely at each end with cotton (Figure 3.4).

The great moment has arrived. Suspend the cross between the poles of the horseshoe — just above is best so that the magnets cannot touch each other. Touch two opposite strips of foil with your battery wires and the cross will swing. Hold the wires steady and the second pair of strips will make contact with them, causing the other arm of the cross to continue the rotary movement as its poles are both attracted and repelled. Now the original pair of foil strips will be making contact with the battery wires again — *but reversed* — and the cross will continue to rotate. You have just constructed an electric motor.

## PRACTICAL STARTER MOTOR

Although we have the basic motor design it needs a great deal of beefing-up before it can turn a cold engine fast enough to get it to fire, and it has to be able to cope with current up to 350 amps.

So instead of our cork we have a *commutator* composed of copper bars moulded into plastic and turned into a drum shape; the iron cross becomes a heavy *armature*; the horseshoe magnet changes into *pole pieces* mounted inside the starter body; the two wires touching the foil strips are now *brushes*, high-pressure moulded from powdered copper and graphite; and the whole unit runs in proper *bearings*. These are the basics, but there are different types of starter motor and also variations in design.

Modern starters, for example, have four brushes and four magnetic pole pieces. This does not affect the basics; it is purely a design feature to give extra power.

Do not worry if your starter does not have a drum commutator: another modern design development is to have a disc or face type commutator. In this, instead of the copper segments being arranged in drum form, they are set radially at the end of the armature and the brushes are pressed against the disc by coil springs. With the older drum type, the brushes are set radially and pressed against the segments by flat coiled springs (Figure 3.5).

One component, although not part of the motor, is essential to it: the *solenoid*. Because of the enormously heavy current

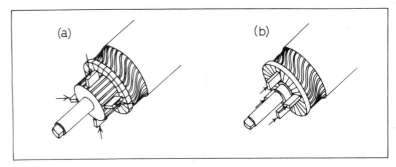

**Figure 3.5** Commutator: (a) drum type, (b) face or disc type

needed to turn the car's engine, to try to pass it through the ignition key switch would simply result in a strong smell of burning from behind the dashboard as the switch melted! So when you turn the key a small flow of current goes to the solenoid, energising its electromagnet, which closes a heavy-duty switch inside. The solenoid is the link between the heavy cable from the battery and the heavy cable to the starter motor.

## STARTER DRIVE

Now we have a powerful motor and a method of switching it, but it still has to be coupled to the engine. There are two main types of starter drive in general use; the *inertia* or *shock* drive, and the *pre-engaged* drive. In both cases, the flywheel of the engine in which they are used is fitted with a toothed ring around the circumference.

The inertia or Bendix drive consists of a heavy toothed pinion that fits loosely on a steel sleeve. The sleeve has spiral grooves machined in it — Figure 3.6(a) — which act as a screw thread, and match a similar thread in the bore of the pinion. The sleeve is fixed to the starter motor shaft and turns with it. When the motor is switched on it accelerates rapidly, but the weight (inertia) of the pinion resists rotation at first, so because of the loose fit the sleeve turns inside the pinion. This action moves the pinion along the thread of the sleeve until it engages the teeth on the flywheel. When fully engaged, the pinion is at the end of the sleeve and has to turn with it, thus turning the flywheel and starting the engine. When the engine fires and picks up speed, the flywheel runs faster than the starter motor and the pinion is 'unscrewed' back along the sleeve and out of mesh with the flywheel.

There are several variations of the Bendix drive, all working on the above principle.

● Earlier starters had a threaded sleeve and pinion as described above, plus a heavy shock or buffer spring. The pinion had a nasty habit of edging along the sleeve until it touched the

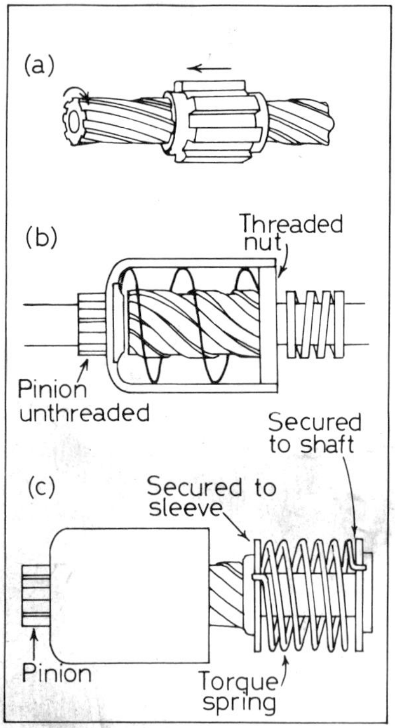

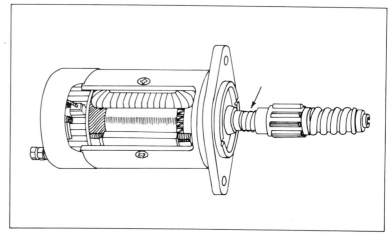

**Figure 3.6** (a) Principle of Bendix drive: when sleeve rotates, pinion's inertia causes it to move along sleeve. (b) Older type. (c) Later type with enclosed retaining spring. (d) Type with torque spring in place of buffer spring

flywheel teeth, so a light spring was fitted to retain the pinion in the disengaged position. See arrow in Figure 3.7.

● A later type of drive uses a lighter pinion, riveted to a hollow steel barrel to give weight. Instead of the thread being machined in the pinion, a threaded ring or nut is secured to the other end of the barrel, and the retaining spring is enclosed in the barrel. See Figure 3.6(b).

● A third type has a torque spring in place of the heavy shock or buffer spring. This is secured by an anchor plate at each end, the inner plate being fixed to the threaded sleeve and the outer one to the shaft. Thus the spring not only absorbs the shock, it also transmits the drive. See Figure 3.6(c).

If the pinion moves towards the starter-motor body on engagement (as in Figure 3.7) it is known as an 'inboard' type; if it moves away from the starter body (as in Figure 3.8) it is an 'outboard' type. This makes no difference to the principle of operation of the drive.

**Figure 3.7** Inertia-drive starter motor

The inertia-drive starter has some obvious drawbacks, especially the violent way the pinion engages the flywheel teeth. This causes damage to both until eventually the pinion jams into the flywheel, locking the engine up solid.

To overcome this problem, more and more modern cars are being equipped with pre-engaged starters. The motor itself is exactly the same as for inertia-type starters, but the drive assembly is different and there is a special solenoid switch mounted on top of the motor. See Figure 3.8.

The solenoid in this case performs two functions. It not only acts as a heavy-duty switch but also, by means of an extension rod and lever, engages the starter pinion before the motor begins to turn. What happens, when the ignition key is turned to the starter position, is that the solenoid is energised and the electromagnetic field set up pulls a plunger towards the switch contacts. At the same time a rod at the end opposite the contact pulls on the lever which moves the

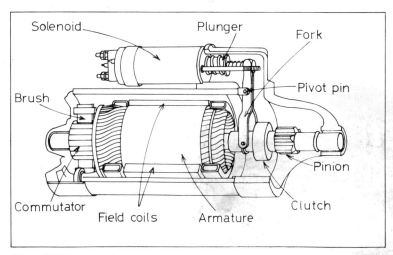

**Figure 3.8** Pre-engaged starter motor

pinion towards the flywheel, and the pinion engages the flywheel teeth fractionally *before* the contacts are closed and the motor begins to turn. The pre-engagement is much kinder to both pinion and flywheel teeth and the whole operation is quieter. But there is, of course, a drawback.

Unlike the inertia drive, which is automatically thrown out when the flywheel outpaces the starter motor, the pre-engaged pinion remains in mesh until the ignition key is released. (Releasing the key de-energises the solenoid, which allows the plunger's return spring to press it back to its original position and, through the lever, draws the pinion out of mesh.) To get over this problem, a free-wheel clutch is incorporated in the drive assembly, but if the key is held too long the clutch can seize up. If this happens the flywheel will cause the starter to over-rev, with disastrous effects on the insides of the motor (see later).

**DISMANTLING THE STARTER**

Although there are many makes of starter this need not worry you. The basic designs of the two types described are similar and only details vary, so dismantling and repairs are much the same for all of them.

Removal of the starter is usually very easy. *First, disconnect the battery*. Next, disconnect the heavy cable from the starter, undo two (normally) or three mounting bolts, and lift the motor away from the clutch housing. You may find on some makes of car that another component gets in the way and has to be removed first, but this does not often happen.

Most starter motors are held together by two long bolts known as 'through bolts'. However, later models with face or disc type commutators have four small screws securing the commutator end bracket, and two short thicker bolts holding the drive end bracket.

To dismantle the unit, first remove the cover band (if fitted), and withdraw the brushes from their holders by hooking up the pressure springs and pulling the brushes free. Remove the nuts and washers from the main terminal, carefully noting the order for reassembly. It's safest to make a rough sketch, because if you get them in the wrong order it could cause trouble.

If your starter has the four small screws holding the commutator end bracket, remove them and pull the bracket clear, lifting the brushes from their slots as you go. Take care that the coil springs don't pop out and get lost.

Remove the through bolts, or the two short bolts from the other type of starter, and the armature can be withdrawn.

The Bendix drive may be secured either by a castellated nut, locked with a split pin, or by a circlip and washer. Hold the armature firmly but not too tightly in a vice, so that the split pin can be extracted and the nut undone — often the nut will have a left-hand thread. If the drive is secured by a circlip, the buffer spring will have to be compressed so that the thrust washer can be moved clear of the circlip to enable you to remove it. You can buy a spring compressor quite cheaply from most good accessory shops, or if you have the patience you could make one from two strong steel plates and a couple of nuts and bolts.

With a starter that has the torque-spring drive, push the outer spring-anchor plate inward and take out the securing pin or circlip. Remove the spring. Push the drive further on to the shaft (you may have to tap it lightly), and remove the key. Now the drive assembly and the end plate can be removed.

With starters that have the pinion and barrel assembly, there is a dished washer inside the barrel at the pinion end with slots in it, and these fit over ribs on the shaft. The slots have to be lined up with the ribs before the barrel can be removed from the shaft.

After dismantling, wash all the parts with petrol and use a small paintbrush to shift the dirt. Dry off well with a clean non-linting cloth. And don't smoke while you are using the petrol!

## FAULT-FINDING AND REPAIR

Most faults on starters are mechanical and can be checked by visual inspection. It is easy to see whether the teeth of the pinion are chewed: if they are, it will have to be renewed by going through the dismantling procedure described above.

Don't forget that, if the pinion is badly worn, the teeth on the flywheel ring gear almost inevitably will be as well. Brushes should have at least 8 mm ($^5/_{16}$ in) left: if they are nearing this limit, renew them. The buffer spring can be checked while the drive assembly is still fully assembled. It should not be possible to rotate the main spring on the shaft by hand. If you can turn it, even slightly, the spring must be replaced.

The bearings should have almost no slack at all. If you can feel movement of the shaft in the bushes, renew them; otherwise as wear increases the armature could spin off-true and knock against the pole pieces, and you might then have to replace the complete unit. The old bearings can be drifted out with hammer and round-rod drift, taking care to support the end bracket securely. New brushes, normally graphite/bronze and obtainable from accessory shops and auto-electricians, should be soaked in engine oil for 24 hours before pressing them into the end brackets. Make sure they enter the holes squarely or they will distort.

If the connection between the main terminal and the field coils is broken, repair is impossible. The coils are formed from aluminium strip and the terminal pressed on, and if the connection breaks, it cannot be soldered. To check the insulation, connect the body of the starter to one terminal of a car battery; then, with your test lamp, join the field-coil terminal to the other battery terminal (Figure 3.9). The bulb should not light. If it does, the insulation has broken down and the field coils (pole pieces) must be removed and the insulation repaired, as follows.

File or saw a small mark on the starter body to show where the terminal is located. Next, remove the screws that hold the pole pieces. They will be very tight indeed, and you will probably need either a shock screwdriver or a hammer and punch to start them. Try not to damage the screw heads too much or you will need new ones when reassembling. Remove the pole shoes and slide out the coils, being very careful of the terminal connection.

The insulation fault will show up as charring. Remove the old, burnt tape carefully and replace it by 13 mm (½ in) tape, which you can get from a draper's shop. Ideally, the new tape should be coated with shellac but this is not absolutely essential. When you replace the pole shoes, the screws must be driven home very tightly; you may have to resort to the hammer and punch again, to get the last fraction of a turn.

To test the armature, connect your test lamp to the battery and shaft, the other battery terminal going to the commutator segments in turn. The bulb should not light.

Check the connections between the windings and the commutator segments for badly soldered joints — usually visible as a gap between the windings and the segments, and signs of overheating at the joint. In really bad cases you can

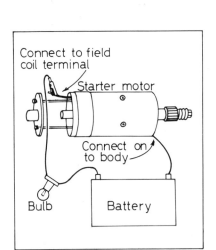

**Figure 3.9** Testing connection between main terminal and field coils

see a ring of sprayed solder around the inside of the starter
body, in line with the commutator connections. Faulty
'insulation' in the armature cannot be repaired and you will
need a replacement.

You can clean dirt from a drum commutator with fine
glasspaper (but use only meths on discs). However, even light
scoring requires skimming in a lathe to true up and to ensure
that the insulation between the segments does not stand
proud. Most small engineering firms or auto-electricians will
do this for you at a small charge.

Brushes worn near to or below 8 mm ($^5/_{16}$ in) should be
replaced. They are usually soldered into place. If your starter
has aluminium field coils (most do), cut the old brush leads,
leaving about 6 mm (¼ in) attached to the coils so that you
can solder the new brush leads to the old 'pigtails'. When you
are reassembling a drum-type commutator starter, hook up
the brush pressure springs and lodge them on the edges of
the holders. Then, after the end plate is back in place, you
can use a small screwdriver to reposition them.

Reassembly is a straightforward reversal of the dismantling
procedure, but check each stage as you go. It is infuriating to
end up with a nice clean motor which, because of a trifling
error along the way, is not working. Before inserting the earth
brushes in their holders on the drum-type commutators,
recheck between the main terminal and the body for insulation
breakdown and rectify any faults before proceeding — the
through bolts can sometimes touch the field-coil connections.

The shaft should be lightly oiled before assembling the
drive, but the spiral grooves on the Bendix sleeve should
*always* be left dry. If you oil it, it will pick up clutch dust and
form a gummy sort of glue that will prevent the pinion from
sliding freely into engagement. In fact, a starter that spins
freely but fails to engage the flywheel may be suffering from
nothing more than this. A quick wash with petrol, without
even dismantling, may cure the trouble.

As far as the motor of the pre-engaged type of starter is
concerned, faults and dismantling are the same as for the
inertia type, except for armature removal. For this the solenoid
has to be taken off first.

Unscrew the nut holding the main starter connection and
the two nuts holding the solenoid to the starter mounting
bracket. Remove the solenoid and unhook the plunger from
the top of the lever.

The pivot pin must now be removed. In some cases this is
simply driven out, other types are screwed in and secured
with a locknut. If the pin is screwed in, the position of the
screw head must be marked with reference to the casting.
This is because some models have a pin with an eccentric
shoulder for adjusting the depth of pinion engagement, so
the pin must be replaced in the same position.

The whole assembly can now be dismantled, and cleaning and testing is the same as for the inertia type of starter.

When reassembling, apply a very light smear of light oil to the solenoid plunger and make sure it can slide freely. Lubricate the lever with engine oil, and also the shaft where the drive assembly slides. When the pinion is in place on the shaft, it should lock solid with the shaft when turned in one direction but turn freely in the opposite direction.

If you find when dismantling either type of starter that the armature windings have spread outwards (usually at the rear end) and have torn the field coils, it is not worth attempting a repair. The cause is over-revving of the starter due to the pinion remaining in mesh with the flywheel. With inertia-type drives, this can be caused by dust and oil gum in the grooves preventing the pinion from disengaging, or something breaking inside the barrel and jamming the pinion in mesh. With pre-engaged starters, the trouble is usually a fault in the ignition switch, or holding the key in the starter position for too long after the engine has fired.

## STARTER FAILURE

Starter motors do not usually give much trouble but, after many years of service, wear on the teeth of the flywheel and the pinion can result in the pinion jamming in mesh. There are two ways to un-jam it. Put the car in third gear and, with the ignition turned off, rock the car. If this fails, put a spanner on the squared end of the armature shaft and turn it — this method will almost always work. Don't forget, however, that this is only a temporary cure; sooner or later it will happen again, and with increasing frequency. The only full cure is to renew the flywheel starter ring and, probably, the Bendix pinion.

A symptom of a jammed pinion is that the engine does not turn, and if you have lights on they will dim. You can get the same symptoms from poor connections, especially at the battery. Although the connection may be good enough to carry current solely for lights, the power needed for the starter will not pass.

Solenoids do not often give trouble, but if you find yours is not closing its contacts when you turn the ignition key there is a get-you-home trick. Some older types of solenoid have a rubber button between the terminals which, if you press it, manually closes the contacts. If there is no button, remove the rubber insulation caps from the terminals and bridge across them with a heavy screwdriver — holding the insulated handle! Unfortunately you cannot use this method on a pre-engaged starter since, although you may get the motor to turn, the lever will not move the pinion into mesh.

In order to ensure a proper earth for the starter, the engine, to which the starter is bolted, has a heavy strap (usually braided copper) bolted to the bodywork. Should this become detached, not only will the starter not function, but the earthing current will try to find another way: if this were something like the choke cable it might become red hot and cause a minor fire.

These dire warnings need not worry you if you carry out the necessary very simple maintenance. The most important thing is to keep all terminals clean and tight, not neglecting the engine earth strap. A 'belt-and-braces' measure is to remove the motor once every 10 000 miles or so and check the brushes, commutator, and Bendix assembly.

# 4 Dynamo

When describing the starter motor we saw how, when a current is passed through a series of coils (the armature) in a magnetic field (the horseshoe magnet or pole pieces), the armature would rotate. The reverse is also true: if a coil, or series of coils, is rotated in a magnetic field, current is generated in the coils.

If we again take the horseshoe magnet, there is a magnetic field between the two ends — the north and south poles. You can't see it but you can prove it exists by a simple experiment. Lay a piece of paper over the horseshoe magnet and sprinkle some iron filings on the paper. Now tap the paper gently and the iron filings will move into a pattern precisely following the lines of force (Figure 4.1) between the magnet's poles.

Now, if a coil consisting of a single turn of wire is rotated in this magnetic field, it will cut the lines of force and a current will be induced in the coil. The more lines of force it cuts per second (or any other unit of time) the higher will be the voltage induced. Therefore the faster it moves, or the stronger the field, the greater the number of lines of force cut and the higher the voltage developed. To go a stage further, if the coil has more than one turn, the number of lines cut will be multiplied by the number of turns and the voltage will be increased proportionally.

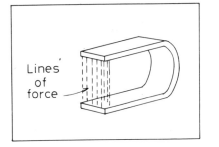

**Figure 4.1** Horseshoe magnet and its magnetic field

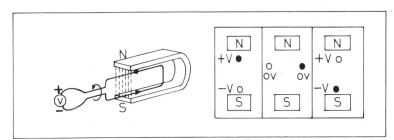

**Figure 4.2** Voltmeter connected in circuit

When a voltmeter is connected to the ends of the coil, you will find that, if the end connected to the top side of the coil is positive, the lower side will be negative (Figure 4.2). But, as the coil rotates, the side that was at the top will become negative as it gets to the bottom, while the negative will

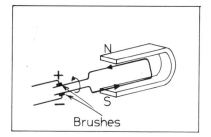

**Figure 4.3** Arrangement of collecters to obtain d.c.

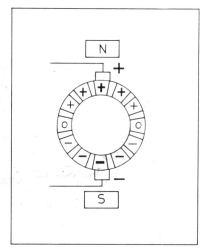

**Figure 4.4** Arrangement used in a starter motor

become positive. There will also be a zero point in each side at mid-position. The result is alternating current (a.c.). But direct current (d.c.) is needed to charge the battery, that is to say current that flows in one direction only. This can be achieved by arranging collectors (brushes) so that they contact each end of the coil alternately (Figure 4.3). The current will be uni-directional, but it will rise and fall from zero to maximum and back again as the coil rotates. As with the starter motor, a series of equally spaced coils can be arranged around the armature, with their ends connected to opposite bars on a commutator, so that there will always be one bar passing through the maximum position while others are moving towards zero and onwards (Figure 4.4).

We now have a continuous flow of direct current, which will increase roughly in direct proportion to the speed of rotation. With a strong permanent magnet this would be fine, except that if the generator were designed to give reasonable output at fairly low speeds it would be giving too much at higher speeds. So we need a way of controlling it.

The stronger the magnetic field, the higher the voltage induced and the higher the current output. Therefore we could control the output by varying the strength of the magnetic field. If, instead of a permanent magnet, we make an electro-magnet by winding a coil of wire round a piece of soft iron, we can vary the strength of the magnet, by varying the current through the coil (Figure 4.5).

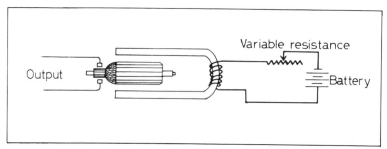

**Figure 4.5** Controlling current output using an electromagnet

In practice, there are usually two coils (called *field windings*) wound around pole shoes inside the generator's body, with the armature rotating between them. At one time, voltage control was done by a third brush that contacted the commutator between the main output brushes. Since the main brushes are mounted at maximum voltage (usually 12 volts) and zero voltage, it follows that any point between them will be at a voltage varying from 12 to zero. If one end of the field winding is connected to the zero brush and the other end to the third brush, the voltage applied to the coil — and therefore

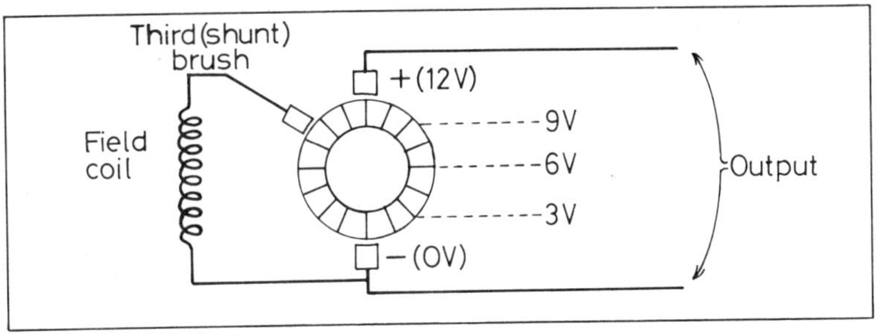

**Figure 4.6** Third-brush system

the strength of the magnetic field — will vary according to the position of the third brush (Figure 4.6).

The third brush (also known as the field brush, shunt brush, or control brush) can be moved, within limits, around the commutator to give the best results for the conditions under which the car is to be used.

The snag with this arrangement used to occur when the car had to be used for short, start-stop trips as well as long continuous journeys. If the brush setting was suitable for short trips it would be too high for the long hauls, and damage to the dynamo and battery could result. If it was right for long journeys it would be too low for short trips and you would soon have had a flat battery. The answer was, of course, to set the field brush to suit every drive! As you would expect, few drivers bothered. Also, as more accessories were added — fog and driving lights, radios, and so forth — load differences could be very great. Some closer, automatic control was therefore needed.

**CONTROL BOX**

Voltage-control problems led to the introduction of the *voltage regulator* (constant voltage control or CVC). The first type was the 'barrel' regulator, which was difficult to maintain and did not remain in use very long before it was superseded by the type that, with modifications, is still in use today.

The basic principle of modern regulators is the same as for the earlier cylindrical type: a variable resistance is inserted in the field circuit to control the dynamo output to suit the state of charge of the battery and the load (lamps, wipers and so on) imposed on the circuit.

The regulator is normally combined with the *cut-out*, which is simply an automatic switch between the battery and dynamo. Together they form what is generally known as the *control box*. In some older cars, fuses to control auxiliary circuits were included in this unit, but nowadays the fuses are contained in a separate fusebox.

## Cut-out

If the battery were to be connected permanently to the dynamo, then when the engine was switched off and the dynamo not charging, the battery would discharge back through the dynamo, which would try to act as a motor. As it would not be powerful enough to turn the engine it would remain stalled and would burn out. To prevent this, the cut-out (or *reverse current relay*, to give it its proper name) is connected into the circuit. In effect it is an automatic switch that closes when the dynamo is in a condition to charge the battery, and opens when the dynamo ceases to charge.

The cut-out consists of a soft iron core with a coil of thin wire wound around it (in other words, an electromagnet). When it is energised, it attracts a spring-loaded armature carrying a contact. This moving contact completes the circuit between battery and dynamo (Figure 4.7).

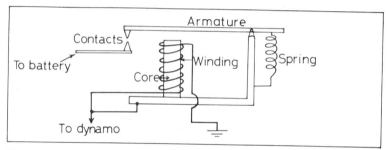

**Figure 4.7** Details of the cut-out (reverse current relay)

The dynamo is *polarised* before use by connecting the field winding temporarily (a couple of seconds is enough) to the 'live' battery terminal. This energises the magnetic pole shoes; then, when the polarising current is removed, although the magnetic field collapses it does not go completely. A small amount of magnetism (known as residual magnetism) remains. When the engine is started the dynamo armature windings cut the weak residual magnetic field, and a very weak current begins to flow through the dynamo field circuit. This strengthens the magnetic field, which in turn increases the current, and so the output voltage is built up. If you have to obtain a replacement unit for any reason, new or second-hand, or if you have left your own in a stripped state for some time, you should carry out the polarising routine before putting the dynamo into service.

The same voltage that is applied to the field coils is also applied to the operating or voltage winding of the cut-out, and this induces a magnetic field in the core of the cut-out. When the voltage builds up to a predetermined value (about 13 to 13.5 volts for a 12-volt system), the magnetism overcomes the spring-loaded armature, pulls it down, and closes

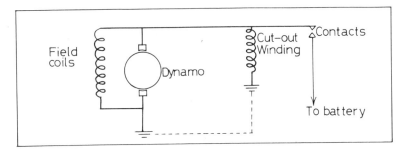

**Figure 4.8** Dynamo circuit with cut-out

the cut-out contacts. Since the dynamo voltage is higher than the battery voltage, current will flow from the dynamo to the battery (Figure 4.8).

When the armature is pulled towards the cut-out core, the gap between them is considerably reduced, but the armature must not actually touch the core or there will be a magnetic lock. To avoid this a small sheet of brass foil is usually fixed over the end of the core or to the underside of the armature; the magnetism required to hold the armature down is then much less than that required to close the contacts.

As the engine slows, the dynamo voltage drops. However, the battery voltage is still sufficient to hold the contacts closed, and the battery begins to discharge back through the dynamo. This, of course, is the last thing we want, so an extra winding is added as follows.

Instead of the connection from the cut-out battery contact being taken straight out, it is connected to a few turns of very thick wire wound over the thin voltage winding. The thick wire is wound in such a way that when the dynamo charge is flowing it generates its own magnetic field in the core, and this helps the voltage winding to keep the contact closed. But when the dynamo voltage drops and the battery current starts to flow back to the dynamo, the heavy reverse current through the thick wire neutralises the magnetic field in the cut-out core, the spring loading takes over, and the contacts open.

The cut-out requires little maintenance. See that the contacts are clean — but go easy on the cleaning, because the contacts are soft metal. Check that the contacts close about halfway through the armature's travel, and ensure that the armature does not come into direct contact with the core.

Adjustment is not normally necessary, but if it is you will need a sensitive d.c. voltmeter. Connect it between the dynamo output terminal and earth, and increase engine revs slowly. The cut-out spring tension is adjusted either by a screw (spring-loaded to prevent it working loose) or a cam, until the contacts close when the dynamo reaches the correct figure. Some Continental cut-outs are adjusted by bending (with a small pair of pliers) a tag that supports the end of the spring blade. This is rather a crude method, and it's not easy to get the correct adjustment. Even a very small bend in the tag makes a big voltage change.

**Voltage regulator**

The regulator works in a similar way to the cut-out, but in reverse. The contacts in their normal state are closed, and energising the magnetic core opens them (Figure 4.9).

When the dynamo starts charging, the voltage builds up as before, but instead of the field current flowing directly around the dynamo circuit, it goes first to the regulator and through

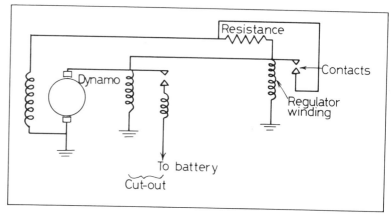

**Figure 4.9** Dynamo circuit with cut-out and voltage regulator

the closed regulator contacts back to the dynamo field. The voltage builds up, the cut-out contacts close, and the dynamo starts charging the battery. If the battery voltage is fairly low, as it will be after starting the engine on the starter motor, the difference between battery and dynamo voltages will be several volts and the charging current will be fairly high. As the engine is revved up the dynamo voltage will increase, as will the difference between dynamo and battery voltages, and also the charging current. This could cause damage to battery and dynamo; the spring tension in the regulator is therefore set so that, at a predetermined dynamo voltage, the regulator contacts open, breaking the field circuit. The field current will stop flowing, the field magnetism will collapse, and the dynamo will stop charging. When the dynamo voltage drops, the contacts close, field current builds up again, voltage increases, and the whole process is repeated.

In practice, a resistance is connected across the regulator contacts. Thus, although the contacts open, the field current is not completely switched off because a small current flows through the resistance. Nevertheless the field current is reduced to the point where the fall in voltage causes the contacts to close again, allowing another build-up of field current.

The resistance has another function. Because the current flow is not completely stopped, it helps to prevent arcing at the contacts, which would cause heating, burning, and eventual failure.

The spring tension, magnetic gaps, and resistance are carefully calculated so that, under any charging conditions, the output voltage of the dynamo is held down to a definite figure. This varies with different types and makes of regulator, but is usually in the region of 15 to 16 volts on open circuit — that is with the connection from the cut-out to the battery disconnected, otherwise the battery voltage would upset the reading.

The regulator contacts become oxidised in use, and if the charge rate drops they should be cleaned with fine emery cloth or a very fine contact file. Before cleaning, use feeler gauges to measure the air gaps between the armature and core,

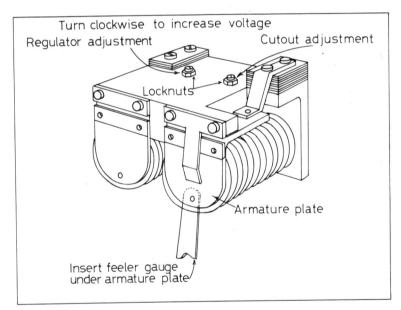

**Figure 4.10** Regulator adjustment

and between the armature and back frame of the unit. You will then be able to check the gaps afterwards, and adjust them if necessary to their original size. This is done by adjusting the screw or cam on Lucas regulators (Figure 4.10), or by carefully bending the armature stop on other types.

If the contacts are very badly burnt, this may be due to failure of the resistance (sometimes visible as a break in the very fine resistance wire on the underside of the unit) or to a partial short in the field windings of the dynamo allowing the field current to be too high.

After cleaning the contacts and checking the air gaps, the voltage setting can be adjusted. First disconnect the cut-out from the battery — or insert a slip of thin card between the cut-out contacts to keep them apart, as shown in Figure 4.10. Run the engine up and adjust the regulator control screw or cam (or bend the tag on Continental types) until the reading on a voltmeter, connected between dynamo output and earth, shows the correct figure.

**Current regulator**

In addition to the cut-out and voltage regulator, many later regulator units have a current control coil, usually the middle one of a three-bobbin control unit (Figure 4.11). It consists of another magnetic core with a few turns of heavy copper

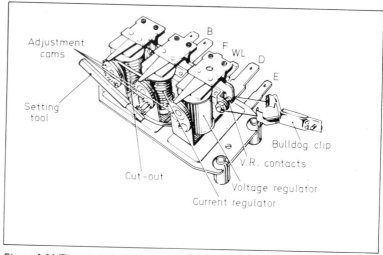

Figure 4.11 Three-bobbin control unit (Lucas RB340)

wire round it. It has a pair of contacts, which are normally closed and connected into the dynamo field circuit in the same way as the voltage regulator.

The heavy wire carries the dynamo output. If this current exceeds a safe value, the magnetic field generated attracts the armature against its spring tension, opening the contacts and reducing the field current.

Maintenance of these contacts is exactly the same as for the voltage-regulator contacts, except that they are adjusted for current flow with the voltage regulator contacts held together, and the output lead to the battery connected.

The current setting should be the maximum rated current for the dynamo, the value of which can be got from maintenance manuals or an auto-electrician. For the majority of British cars fitted with a Lucas C40 dynamo the value is 22 amps. This would be an average setting for most cars except those with special equipment and larger dynamos.

## DYNAMO FAULT-FINDING AND REPAIR

The main cause of dynamo failure is wear and tear. The brushes wear down until the springs can no longer hold them in contact with the commutator, with consequent arcing and burning of the copper segments of the commutator. The heat developed can also cause the soldered joints between windings and commutator bars to melt, resulting in open circuits and a dynamo that no longer charges.

Bearing wear can also cause failure, particularly if an over-tight fan belt has exerted excessive side thrust on the bush in the commutator end bracket, allowing the core of the armature windings to rub against the pole shoes, overheating and burning the insulation.

Another source of trouble is water getting into the dynamo, rotting the tape binding of the field coils and allowing them to short out to the yoke or pole shoes.

Most dynamos are held together by two long bolts that pass right through the unit and clamp the two end plates to the yoke. Usually the drive-end plate (bracket) has tapped

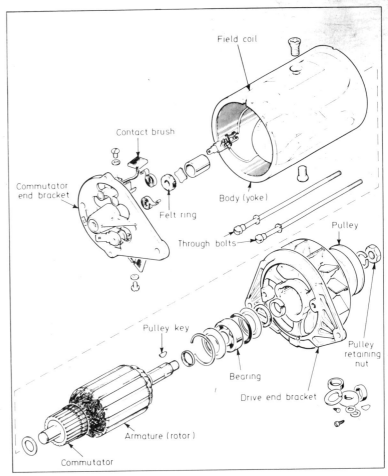

**Figure 4.12** Exploded view of typical dynamo (Lucas C40—1)

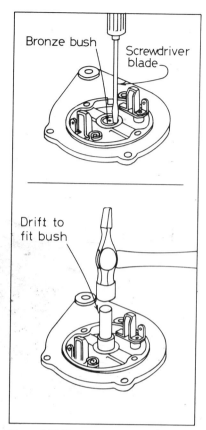

**Figure 4.13** Fitting commutator end bush

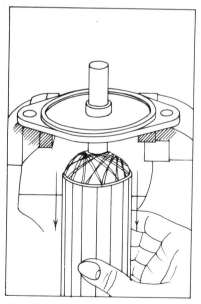

**Figure 4.14** Removing armature from end bracket

holes to screw into, but in some cases the bolts go right through and are secured by nuts.

Remove the two bolts. The drive end bracket complete with armature can then be withdrawn from the yoke, and the commutator end bracket can be removed (Figure 4.12).

On some Bosch dynamos, a small screw securing the field windings to the brush gear must be removed first. On some other types, there are wires between the brush gear and terminals on the yoke that must be disconnected when the end bracket has been partially withdrawn.

Excessive bush wear, or a noisy drive end bearing, mean replacement. The commutator end bush can be removed by slitting it down one side with a small cold chisel or old screwdriver, and then collapsing it. The new bush should be soaked in engine oil for 24 hours before installing. Tap it home gently and squarely using a wooden drift, or press it into place in a vice with a block of wood to protect it (Figure 4.13).

To remove the drive end bearing the armature must be separated from the bracket. Undo the nut securing the pulley and remove the pulley by levering it off with two screwdrivers. Occasionally, a puller has to be used: be careful with this, as pulleys can be easily damaged. Remove the key from the shaft. If you tap the inner end down with a small punch, the outer end will lift and the key can be levered out. Properly speaking, the shaft should be pressed out of the bearing, but . it can be driven out: replace the nut a few turns to protect the threads and use a soft hammer, or interpose a block of wood if you are using a steel hammer (Figure 4.14). The bearing is secured by rivets, screws, or a circlip. Remove these — rivets will have to be drilled out — and the assembly can then be dismantled, but take careful note of the order in which the various washers and seals are arranged. Pack the new bearing with high-melting-point (HMP) grease before installing it.

If the armature has been rubbing the pole shoes because of commutator end bush wear, it will probably be beyond any repair you can make and a replacement unit is the answer. You can fit an exchange dynamo, or you could get a second-hand one from a breaker and overhaul that. You could even build one unit out of two.

Check for 'shorts' to earth, as with the starter armature and field coils (see page 25). Field coil earthing can usually be rectified by removing the coils, re-taping, and coating with shellac varnish. An armature with windings down to earth, however, is beyond repair except by a specialist.

If the soldered joints between windings and commutator have thrown their solder — shown by a ring of sprayed solder round the inside of the yoke — they can, with care, be cleaned and resoldered. Use cored solder, not spirit flux; you will need

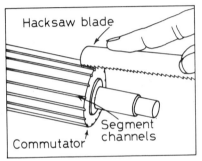

**Figure 4.15** Cleaning and undercutting commutator segments

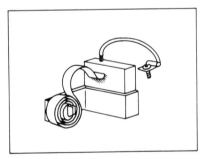

**Figure 4.16** Refitting the commutator end bracket, supporting the brushes

a large soldering iron, preferably one of the old gas-heated type, since you will have to solder a fairly large mass of copper, which will conduct heat away very quickly.

A commutator that is only discoloured can be cleaned with a strip of fine glasspaper (Figure 4.15), but if it is at all burnt it must be skimmed in a lathe to true it up.

After skimming, the insulation between the commutator segments must be undercut. Left level, the softer copper will wear away and the insulation will stand proud; eventually the brushes will be bounced clear of the copper, arcing and burning, with the result that finally the brushes will not make contact and the dynamo will stop generating. The insulation is best undercut with an old hacksaw blade that has had the 'set' ground off to make it straight, like a serrated knife (Figure 4.15). It should not be ground to a knife edge, however: the tips of the teeth should be square and approximately the width of the groove to be cut. The insulation should be undercut to a depth of about 1 mm ($^1/_{32}$ in). Remove any burrs.

Reassembly of the dynamo is simply the reverse of dismantling. Make sure the brushes slide freely in their holders. Any tightness should be eased by rubbing them on a fine file or glasspaper stretched over a block.

When replacing the bracket, hold the brushes in the holders but clear of the commutator by allowing the tips of the springs to press against the sides of the brushes (Figure 4.16). Put a smear of oil on the armature shaft before inserting it into the bush.

After the dynamo is reassembled, lever the springs on to the tops of the brushes with a small screwdriver inserted through the holes in the end bracket. If there are no holes, the springs should be eased into position through the gap between bracket and yoke just before the bracket is pushed right home. Insert the through bolts and tighten up, making sure the bolts do not foul any connections inside and that the end brackets are fully home in the yoke.

The dynamo can be checked by connecting it to a battery and running it as a motor. Most dynamos have one end of the field coils connected to the yoke, and can be tested by connecting one terminal of the battery to the casing or one end bracket, joining both dynamo terminals together and to the other battery terminal. The armature should spin smoothly with a fair amount of torque.

If the inner end of the field coil is connected to the 'live' brush, as is the case with some Continental units, the field terminal should be connected to the frame and one battery terminal; the large output terminal goes to the other battery post.

Always connect the dynamo to the battery with the same polarity it will have in the car. For the dynamo from a car

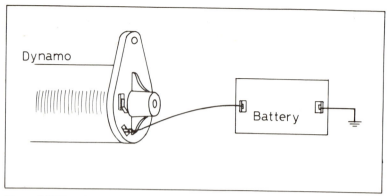

**Figure 4.17** Repolarising a dynamo

with negative earth, the yoke should be connected to the negative battery terminal, and vice versa. In any case, the dynamo should always be polarised as a precaution when it has been refitted to the car: before connecting it up, take an odd length of wire, connect between the field terminal and the live battery terminal for about two seconds, and the job is done (Figure 4.17).

## ROUTINE CHECKS

A much neglected but vitally important maintenance job is keeping the fan belt at the correct tension. A loose belt is a short path to a flat battery, and one that is overtight puts excessive strain on dynamo bearings. The usual recommendation is that there should be 13—20 mm (½—¾ in) deflection in the belt's longest run.

Two instruments that are extremely useful for keeping a check on the charging system are an ammeter and a battery condition indicator. The ammeter shows the amps being discharged or charged at any given moment, and the battery condition indicator shows the battery voltage when the ignition is switched on and the generator voltage when the engine is running. Both these instruments are described fully in Chapter 8.

An important point about control-box maintenance (apart from occasionally checking the contacts, as described earlier) is to ensure that the clip-on lid is not cracked or broken. The unit is very sensitive to temperature — as it is designed to be, since bi-metallic strips vary the tension on the armatures — and a damaged lid will not maintain the desired temperature range.

At infrequent intervals, say once a year, remove the control box from the bulkhead and check to see if there is any dirt or dampness to affect the resistors under the base plate.

# 5 Alternator

At reasonable engine speeds and for electrical systems with a modest current demand, the d.c. generator or dynamo is quite satisfactory. But with more modern engines running at higher revs and with extra electrical equipment, the dynamo has limitations. To generate the extra current demanded, the physical size of the armature, and therefore of the complete generator, has to be increased until the weight and size become excessive. Also, at higher revs the armature windings have a tendency to throw outwards under centrifugal force and can, in extreme cases, burst with disastrous results. Another drawback is that, with increased current output, there is increased wear between brushes and commutator.

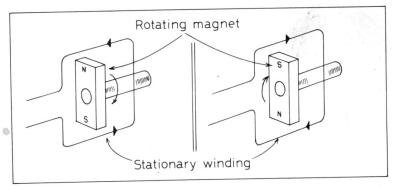

**Figure 5.1** Principle of the alternator: as the magnet (rotor) rotates, the current is continually reversed

Whereas the dynamo consists of a series of coils rotating in a magnetic field, the alternator is something like a dynamo 'inside out', i.e. a magnetic field rotating inside a series of coils (Figure 5.1). This brings several advantages.

● The rotating magnet (rotor), which is an electromagnet with a variable strength (as in the dynamo field coils), can be made strong enough to rotate at much higher speeds without danger. The field windings contain a relatively small amount of wire, so the hazard of damage from centrifugal force is minimised.
● The field current is low; so, although there must be contact brushes to conduct the current to the field windings, there is very little brush wear.

• The main windings, being fixed, can be made much heavier, and as they are embedded in the *stator* (an assembly of iron rings with slots, fitted to the yoke — see Figure 5.2) they keep much cooler than in the dynamo armature; therefore a higher output is possible for the same unit weight.

Thus, since the alternator can be run faster at higher engine revs, it automatically runs faster than a dynamo at low revs.

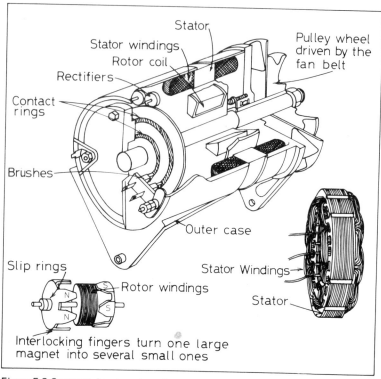

Figure 5.2 Cutaway drawing of an alternator

The dynamo only starts charging the battery when the car is doing about 40 km/h (25 mile/h), but an alternator can deliver a useful amount of current in heavy traffic at low speeds.

The field current is conveyed to the rotor windings by brushes in contact with two *slip rings*. Since there is no commutator to reverse the field, the current generated in the main windings reverses with each half-revolution of the rotor, giving alternating current.

Until recently, the conversion to direct current needed for charging the battery was done by rather bulky metal rectifiers mounted away from the generator, not unlike the control box for a dynamo. Modern alternators, however, use semi-conductor diodes as rectifiers; although small, these can handle quite large currents and can be built into the alternator. The diode can be regarded as an electrical non-return valve, i.e. it will pass current in one direction only. Thus the generated current, which flows first in one direction and then the other, has the reverse current blocked by the diode. The result is a uni-directional current, in pulses.

Output control is similar to that of d.c. generators. It is achieved by varying the strength of the field current, the regulator ('control unit') doing this automatically. Many Continental alternators use an electromagnetic regulator similar to that used to control dynamo output, but the Lucas system uses transistorised components. These are small assemblies sealed in resin and virtually impossible to adjust or repair.

Earlier alternators (10AC and 11AC) had the regulator as an external fitting, usually mounted with a field-energising relay and a warning-light control unit. Later types (15ACR, 16ACR, 17ACR etc.) have the regulator built into the alternator, making it a self-contained unit.

When the battery is low, a transistorised regulator allows the full field current to pass through it. Then, as battery voltage rises, the regulator gradually reduces the field current and so reduces the alternator output. If a load is applied by switching on lights, wipers, heated rear window or similar equipment, the battery voltage drops slightly and the regulator compensates by allowing more field current to flow — almost like opening a tap — and the alternator output increases to compensate for the additional load. When the load is switched off, the alternator output is correspondingly reduced.

**WARNING:** a big danger with alternators is damage through a wrongly connected battery. Unlike the dynamo, which is isolated from the battery when at rest by the cut-out, the output terminal of an alternator is permanently connected to the 'live' battery terminal. When charging is not taking place, current cannot flow from the battery through the alternator because the main diodes will only allow current to pass in one direction: from the alternator to the battery. If, however, the battery is wrongly connected, the electrical pressure on the diodes is reversed and a heavy current will flow — much heavier than the controlled output of the alternator. A great deal of heat will then be generated inside. This will damage the diodes and windings and render the unit useless — and it does not take very long to do it.

## MAINTENANCE AND FAULT-FINDING

There is very little routine maintenance on an alternator. The slip-ring brushes should be inspected from time to time and replaced when worn, and the slip rings themselves should be kept clean.

If the ignition warning light fails to go out when the engine is running, probably the generator is not functioning. However, the Lucas 10AC and 11AC alternator circuits have the peculiarity that the warning light can stay on while the alternator is actually charging.

The warning-light control is a small unit in the circuit, looking very similar to the older type of cylindrical flasher unit. Actually, it is a small relay with its contacts normally closed. The warning-light circuit is from the ignition switch to the warning light, then from the light through the relay contacts to earth. This lights the lamp when the engine is switched on. When the alternator starts to charge the battery, a small current from a separate terminal on the alternator energises the relay, which opens the contacts, breaks the warning-light circuit, and thus puts out the light (Figure 5.3).

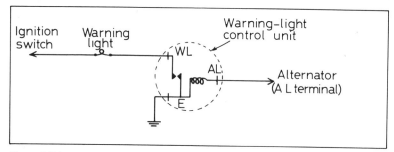

Figure 5.3 Lucas 10AC and 11AC alternator warning-light circuit

Failure of the warning light to come on when the ignition is switched on can be due to bulb failure or to a fault in the warning-light control. Check by connecting the warning-light control WL terminal to earth: if the bulb lights the control unit is at fault.

If the warning light does not go out when the alternator is charging, it may be due to failure of the warning-light control or failure of the circuit from the alternator to the warning-light control. A voltmeter connected between the AL terminal of the alternator and earth should show a reading of about 7 volts.

To test the alternator and regulator unit, go through the following routine.

1. Switch on the ignition but do not start the engine.
2. Remove the field supply wire from the alternator (usually brown/purple or brown/white). Test for current by connecting your test lamp between the end of the wire and earth. If it lights, go to step 5.
3. If the lamp does not light, carry out the following test. The field supply wire is connected at the other end either

to a relay or to the ignition switch. If a relay is fitted, check between the output terminal (brown/white wire) and earth (Figure 5.4). If this is 'live', the fault is in the wire between relay and alternator. The same type of check should be made if the wire is connected to the ignition switch.

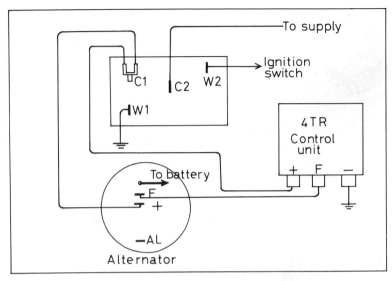

**Figure 5.4** Alternator circuit for testing

4. If the previous test is not 'live', check the input to the relay (brown wire), usually from the live terminal on the starter solenoid. Where this gives a positive result, check the white wire, which operates the relay, connected to the ignition switch. If this, too gives a positive (live) reaction, check the earth connection (black wire). If this is in order, the fault must lie in the relay unit.
5. Having found that the field supply wire is 'live', reconnect it to its terminal and remove the other field wire (brown/green) that goes to the regulator unit. When you connect your test lamp between the vacant field terminal and earth, it should light; go to step 7. If if does not, the fault is in the alternator field circuit.
6. Take out the screws securing the brush holder and remove it. Then check that the brushes protrude well clear of the holder, and can move freely (Figure 5.5). Worn brushes must be replaced, then you can re-test. If the brushes are sound, the fault is in the rotor and the alternator will have to be replaced or repaired.
7. If the lamp lights when carrying out step 5, replace the wire and check for current at the F terminal of the regulator, with the earth connection off. Failure of the lamp to light means that the fault is in the wire between alternator and

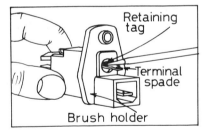

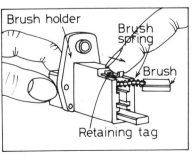

**Figure 5.5** Checking brushes for wear

regulator. Should the bulb light, you must check for continuity between the F and — (negative) terminals of the regulator. To do this, remove the wires from the regulator, earth the negative terminal, and connect the test lamp between the 'live' battery terminal and the F terminal of the regulator. Failure to light means that the regulator is faulty.

8. If the field and regulator circuits are working correctly, the alternator itself is at fault and will have to be removed for examination.

The alternator is held together by three long bolts spaced round the body of the unit. Remove the three bolts, and the nuts securing the main terminal; the three main parts can then be separated.

As you remove the brush holder you can check the brushes and decide if they require renewal. Inspect the slip rings for signs of burning or unevenness. If not too bad they can be cleaned with a light abrasive, but should they be scored they must be skimmed true in a lathe. This job is best left to an expert because there is little metal to play with. Check for current continuity with a battery and test lamp (Figure 5.6): no light means a break in the winding or a badly soldered joint where the wire joins the slip ring. Also, check for short circuits to the core or shaft. If the main stator windings are burnt or shorting to earth, they are usually beyond repair.

To check the main diodes with the test lamp, first connect the negative battery terminal to the body of the unit. Next, connect one test lead to the positive battery terminal and the other to the output terminal of the alternator. The lamp should not light. Now reverse the battery connections so that the positive is connected to the body and the negative to the test lamp. The lamp should light. Any other result means that the diodes are faulty.

There are three series of overlapping windings in the stator, and to check the individual windings they must be disconnected from the diodes. The soldered joints have to be broken, and later resoldered; this also has to be done if the diodes are to be replaced. The latter job is not as simple as it may sound as the diodes are very easily damaged by heat, and if the soldering iron is held in contact with the terminal for too long the diode can be damaged. Conversely, when resoldering, if the iron is not held in contact for long enough a 'dry' joint will result, which will fail in service. The possibility of heat damage can be minimised by holding the diode terminal in the jaws of a large pair of pliers, to draw away the heat while the soldering is done (Figure 5.7).

Generally speaking, however, if rotor, diodes or stator windings are faulty, it is better to fit a replacement alternator.

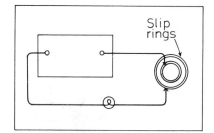

Figure 5.6 Testing the rotor windings for continuity

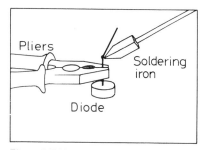

Figure 5.7 Method of soldering diodes

**ACR ALTERNATORS**

The construction of ACR alternators is very similar to the AC range, except that a metal rectifier is used instead of diodes to convert the alternating current to direct current needed to charge the battery. Also the regulator unit is incorporated in the alternator.

Another difference is that the bearing at the slip ring end of the rotor is mounted behind the slip ring, which has to be disconnected and taken off before the bearing can be removed. This is a very delicate task and should not be attempted unless absolutely necessary.

Service and maintenance is the same as for AC alternators. But remember, always disconnect the battery before doing electrical work of any description, except circuit testing.

# 6 Ignition

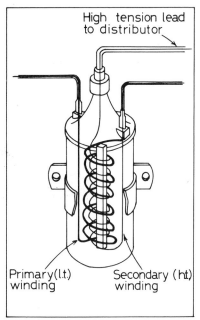

High tension lead to distributor

Primary (l.t.) winding

Secondary (h.t.) winding

**Figure 6.1** Ignition coil in section

## IGNITION COIL

The principle of the four-stroke petrol engine is fairly simple. A piston moves down a cylinder, sucking in a petrol and air mixture. It moves up again, compressing the mixture, which is at some point ignited by a spark. Then it is forced down under the pressure of the burning gas, and finally up again to get rid of the burnt gas. The object of the ignition system is to provide the spark at precisely the right time during the four-stroke cycle; the timing varies according to engine design, engine revs, and the load. The system has not only to generate and time the high-voltage sparks between the electrodes of the sparking plugs, it also has to distribute them to the cylinders in the correct firing sequence. The ignition system copes with all this with remarkable reliability, unless neglected, which all too often it is.

We have seen how important a magnetic field is to starter motor, generator, solenoid, and control units. We now come to another, equally important, application: the *ignition coil* (Figure 6.1).

If a soft-iron core has a coil of wire wound round it and an electric current is passed through the wire, the iron core will become a magnet. Now, if we wind a second coil of wire on to the same iron core, when the current is passed through the first winding a magnetic field will build up, and when the current ceases the field will collapse. In the process of increasing and collapsing, the magnetic field *moves* in relation to the second winding and thus generates a momentary current in it. (Remember how the dynamo and alternator generate current by the movement of a winding in the presence of a magnetic field, and vice versa.) As we shall see, in the case of the ignition coil it is the collapse of the field that is made use of.

The purpose of including the second winding is that the momentary voltage induced in it has a direct relationship with the number of turns of wire in each of the coils. For instance, suppose that the first winding (primary) has 100 turns of wire and the second coil (secondary) has 1000 turns: if a 12 volt supply is passed through the primary windings, the voltage induced in the secondary winding will be increased tenfold to 120 volts. By increasing the ratio between the two windings, the secondary voltage will be still further built up, which is how the coil produces the necessary voltage for the high-tension spark needed to ignite the mixture in the cylinders. To enable the coil to generate the sparks, we need the aid of the *distributor*, which also arranges to deliver them to the right cylinder at the right time.

**DISTRIBUTOR**

Basically, the distributor consists of two separate parts: a mechanical switch to energise the low-tension (primary) winding of the coil at appropriate intervals, and a rotary

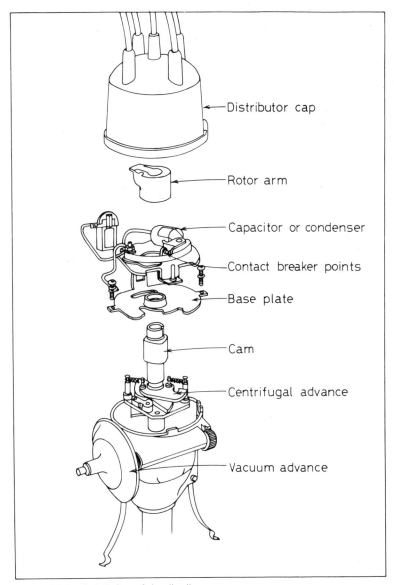

Figure 6.2 Exploded view of the distributor

switch to distribute the high-tension spark generated to the appropriate sparking plug (Figure 6.2).

## Contact breaker

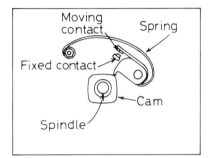

**Figure 6.3** Operation of the contact breaker

The mechanical switch, known as the *contact breaker,* is operated by a spindle driven by gears from the engine's camshaft. Fitted to the spindle is a cam with one lobe for each cylinder. As the cam rotates, each lobe in turn presses against a fibre block (later nylon was used) attached to the moving part of a pair of contacts. The moving contact is spring loaded to hold it against the cam. As the contacts open and close, the current to the low-tension winding of the coil is switched on and off (Figure 6.3). Each time the contacts open, the magnetic field collapses and a high voltage is induced in the secondary windings of the coil.

When a pair of contacts carrying an electric current are separated, the current tries to keep flowing and this causes arcing between the contact faces. For most components on the car (lighting switches and so on) the switching is fairly infrequent and it takes a very long time before the arcing burns the contacts seriously; but distributor contact-breaker points operate very rapidly and continuously, so serious burning and heating can occur.

With voltage-regulator contacts, as we saw in Chapter 4, burning is reduced by the resistance connected across the contacts in the dynamo field circuit. The circuit is not completely broken when the contacts open as the resistance offers an alternative path. However, in the distributor we want a complete break of circuit, so another device is used to quench the arcing — the *condenser.*

The condenser is connected across the contacts in such a way that, when they open, the current that would have continued to flow for a fraction of a second, in the form of an arc across the contact gap, is diverted into the condenser; this then becomes 'charged', and little or no spark occurs at the points. But the current immediately flows out again, as if it were driven by a spring, and the only way it can go is back through the coil in the reverse direction.

As the contacts open and switch off the primary current, the magnetic field starts to collapse, and in doing so induces a high-tension voltage to build up in the secondary windings. When the reverse current from the condenser starts to flow through the primary winding, it forces the field to collapse even more rapidly. We have seen previously that the faster the coils of a generator cut the lines of force, the higher the voltage generated. In a similar way, the faster the coil magnetic field collapses, the higher the voltage induced in the secondary winding. The condenser, therefore, not only reduces sparking at the contacts, it also boosts the high-tension voltage.

**Rotor arm**

Having got the high-voltage spark, the next thing is to deliver it to each plug in turn at the right time.

Since the spindle is rotating at the correct speed to generate the right number of sparks, the same spindle rotation can also be used to distribute the sparks to the plugs (Figure 6.4). A heavily insulated rotor arm mounted on top of the spindle

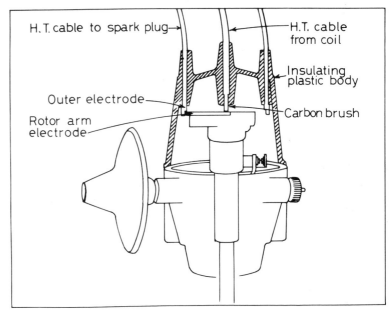

Figure 6.4 Rotor arm and contacts in distributor cover

carries a brass electrode on its upper surface. Evenly spaced around the inner surface of the distributor cap, which is made from insulating material, are a number of electrodes (studs), one for each cylinder. The electrodes are carried through the cover to terminals on the outside.

A centre terminal in the distributor cap receives the high-tension current from the coil and, by means of a spring-loaded carbon brush or a carbon pad that contacts a spring collector on the rotor itself, conducts the high-tension current to the brass electrode on the rotor. As the rotor revolves, the outer end of the rotor electrode passes very close to — but not actually touching — the studs spaced around the cap.

The design of the distributor ensures that, as the rotor passes each stud electrode, the cam on the spindle opens the contacts and causes the high-tension current to be generated in the coil. The pulse passes from the coil to the rotor, along the rotor electrode to the appropriate stud, through the high-tension lead connected to it externally to the sparking plug, where it jumps the gap between the plug electrodes as a spark and, one hopes, ignites the mixture in the cylinder.

**Centrifugal advance**

So now we have the distributor and coil generating and distributing nice fat sparks to the plugs in the right order and at the right time, and the engine can be started. However, if the engine revs are then increased, the spark will be occurring at the wrong time! This is because of the time (although infinitesimal) taken for the flame front to spread through the mixture. As engine revs increase, the spark is needed earlier and earlier to allow for the flame-spread delay and to derive the full benefit from the gas pressure developed.

In early motoring days this was done by turning the whole distributor by means of a hand-operated lever. If the distributor is rotated slightly in the opposite direction to the rotation of the spindle, the contact-breaker 'heel' will meet the cam lobes earlier and the ignition timing will be advanced.

Although this was quite effective it did not get the best performance from the engine because of the need constantly to adjust the advance and retard to suit revs, something that was not a practical possibility. And if the ignition was inadvertently left advanced when starting the engine, the resulting 'kick-back' when it fired could — and did — damage the starter motor; it was not unknown for the starter shaft to bend or even break. If the engine was being cranked with a starting handle, the driver could easily break his wrist. In fact,

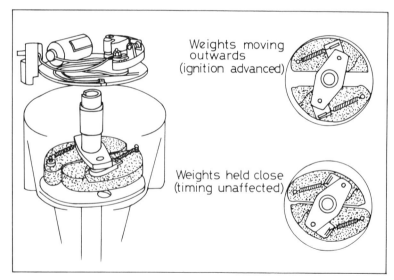

**Figure 6.5** Centrifugal advance and retard

there was a technique, as veteran and vintage car owners will know, of keeping one's thumb away from the handle when cranking so that, if there was a 'kick-back', the handle would be torn from one's grasp rather than damaging the wrist! So the automatic advance mechanism was introduced.

The centrifugal advance system, as most commonly used, consists of a cam which, instead of being fixed to the distributor spindle, as with earlier models, is made in the form of a sleeve that fits over the top of the spindle and can rotate round it (Figure 6.5). It is held in position by an arrangement of pivoted weights and springs; as the speed of the spindle's rotation increases, the weights swing outwards against the tension of the springs. As the weights move outwards, the linkage connecting them to the cam moves it in relation to the spindle, thus advancing the ignition timing. As engine revs decrease, the springs take over and return the weights (and therefore the cam) to their original positions.

The overall movement of the weights (bob weights) is calculated so that the maximum movement matches the engine characteristics, and spring tension is arranged to give the correct degree of advance over the effective range of the engine. Every engine has its own characteristics and needs a distributor with an advance range to suit it, so distributors are not interchangeable between different types of engine.

**Vacuum advance**

Having developed an effective system of automatic advance, it was realised that, when cruising in top gear at comparatively low revs, i.e. when the automatic advance was not at its maximum, the engine could stand a few more degrees advance, provided this could be immediately retarded when the throttle was opened. Thus the vacuum advance was added (Figure 6.6).

When the pistons draw the mixture into the cylinders, a partial vacuum is set up in the inlet manifold. This partial vacuum is not constant: when the throttle is closed it is high,

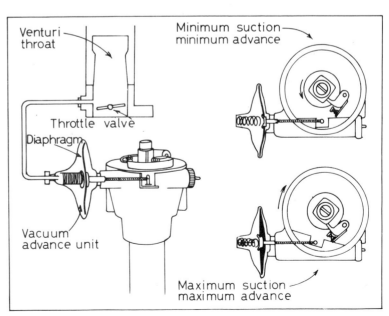

**Figure 6.6** Vacuum advance and retard

but immediately the throttle is opened and air rushes in, the vacuum drops. This is just what is wanted for the extra advance system.

A small capsule containing a diaphragm is fitted to the outside of the distributor. One side of the diaphragm is connected by a tube to the inlet manifold so that, when the vacuum is high, the diaphragm is pulled towards the manifold against a spring tension. The other side of the diaphragm is connected to the distributor base plate, which carries the contact-breaker points and which can rotate about the distributor spindle between stops. When the vacuum increases, the mechanism will advance the timing, but when the throttle is opened and the vacuum reduced, the return spring will retard it.

Although the basic design is the same in principle, distributors vary in design detail. For example, bob weights for centrifugal advance are usually fitted below the contact-breaker plate, but some (such as AC Delco and Marelli) have them fitted to the spindle above the contacts. There are other variations, but none that should cause confusion.

## MAINTENANCE

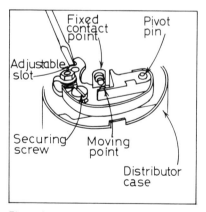

Figure 6.7 Adjusting the contact breaker gap

Distributor maintenance is straightforward. Firstly, keep things clean. High-tension current always takes the line of least resistance; if it can by-pass the circuit by going to earth down, for instance, a damp distributor cap, it will do so. A crack in the cap will also have the same effect, even if dry, because the carbonisation accumulated gives an easy track to earth. A temporary cure may be to scrape out the carbonised crack with the tip of a small screwdriver, and scoring across it to act, as it were, as a fire-break. This is not a permanent cure, and a replacement cap should be fitted as soon as possible.

Contact-breaker points should be kept to the correct gap — you will find this in the owner's handbook or by reference to the manufacturer. The procedure for gapping points is shown in Figure 6.7. If they are discoloured, clean them with fine-grade glasspaper; better still, file them flat with a warding file so that the faces meet accurately. Opinions vary about when points should be renewed, and a lot depends upon the conditions under which they have to work. They could carry on for 16 000 or even 24 000 km (10 000 or 15 000 miles), but to be really safe change them at 10 000 km (6000 mile) intervals. If you do you are far less likely to suffer ignition troubles.

Another neglected service is distributor lubrication. A smear of Vaseline on the spindle cam minimises contact-breaker 'heel' wear, not only prolonging the life of the points but also helping to maintain the correct gap. Centrifugal advance weights should also be kept oiled. In some cases they are mounted below the rotor and easy to get at, in others (Lucas) there are holes in the base plate; sometimes you may have to detach the base plate — two or three screws — to give access.

Should it be necessary to renew the bob-weight advance springs because they have stretched or lost their tension, replacements are normally available from manufacturers' agents. Make sure you get the correct ones for your particular distributor, and note carefully how the originals are fitted before you remove them. The two springs are not always identical, and very often one is heavier than the other. The lighter spring gives a quick advance of a few degrees at the lower range of engine revs; the heavier spring then takes over to give a slower rate of advance through the rest of the rev range.

When fitting a new contact set, make sure you know just where the insulating washers and terminal tags go. Misplacing them is very likely to prevent them working.

High-tension leads are of two types: wire-cored, which must be fitted with suppressor caps at the plug end to avoid interference on radios and televisions, and the now almost universal graphite-cored leads, which are self-suppressing. Wire-cored leads only need replacing if the insulation shows signs of perishing, but graphite-cored leads should be replaced after 12 months or so, since the core can break down and cause misfiring at the plugs.

**Dwell meters**

Most owners, when setting the contact-breaker gap, will depend upon a feeler gauge with the 'heel' on one cam lobe only. This is usually a satisfactory method, although it is better to check each lobe separately and average out. But in recent times it has become common practice to use a dwell meter to check contact-gap settings.

The measurement of the contact gap will have been calculated to give the correct ratio of contacts closed to contacts open, to allow the coil sufficient time to build up an effective magnetic field. The dwell meter simply measures the number of degrees through which the distributor cam rotates while the points are closed. The advantage of the dwell meter is that it takes into consideration any wear on distributor cam lobes (this is very important: wear might have an effect on coil magnetic field recovery), so that an average points gap setting can be made.

The intermittent current flow through the contact-breaker circuit gives a series of impulses to the dwell-meter needle, which takes up a position showing the average values of these impulses. If the gap setting is correct and the wear in the distributor is within the allowed tolerance, the reading on the scale will be correct for that particular model of distributor at the prescribed engine speed — variations of engine speed will affect the reading. Any departure from the recommended figures should be corrected by slight adjustment of the contact-breaker gap.

## Removing the distributor

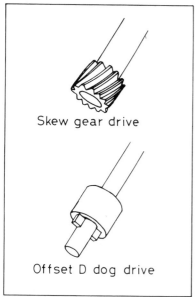

Skew gear drive

Offset D dog drive

Figure 6.8 Skew gear and offset 'D' dog drive

## Ignition timing

On some cars the distributor is rather inaccessible and it is easier to set the points gap by removing it from the engine. If you do so, turn the engine over until No.1 piston is on the compression stroke, and mark the distributor flange and the cylinder block as a reference for re-installation. Take off the distributor cap, and mark the position of the rotor arm on the distributor casing. Unless you have to retime the ignition, do not touch the clamp bolt; undo the two bolts that secure the flange to the block and withdraw the unit. If the distributor shaft has skew-gear drive on it (Figure 6.8), the rotor arm will turn a little as you withdraw the unit. Mark on the distributor casing how much movement there has been so that you can replace it correctly.

If you position the rotor arm at the second mark, as the drive engages the camshaft the arm should move round so that it is lined up with the first mark when the distributor is fully home. It only remains to ensure that the flange and block marks are also lined up; you can then replace the securing bolts and the timing should not have been disturbed. With offset 'D' drive (Figure 6.8) a similar procedure is followed.

Retiming the ignition is not the daunting task it might seem to be if you follow a simple procedure.

Most engines are timed on No.1 cylinder — you can check this in the handbook, which will also tell you the correct number of degrees before t.d.c. (top dead centre, i.e. when the piston is at the top of its travel on the compression stroke) that the spark should occur. If you remove No.1 sparking plug and turn the engine over with a spanner on the crankshaft pulley nut, you can feel with a pencil when the piston arrives at t.d.c. In this position, the timing marks should be lined up as for t.d.c. These marks are either on the crankshaft pulley — with a pointer on the block — or on the block with a notch in the pulley (Figure 6.9). With most transverse engines, the marks are on the flywheel: you will have to remove a cover plate on the flywheel housing and view the marks with a torch, using a mirror to enable you to see inside the housing.

Now turn the engine round again until the timing piston is again on the compression stroke. Line up the correct timing mark on the pulley to the correct number of degrees before t.d.c., making sure that the rotor arm is pointing at the electrode in the distributor cap for No. 1 cylinder. Now, connect your test lamp to the distributor low-tension terminal and earth. Switch on the ignition and slacken the clamp bolt so as to allow the distributor to be turned easily. Keeping the

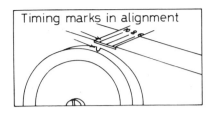

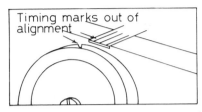

**Figure 6.9** Ignition timing marks

**Spark plugs**

rotor steady, rotate the distributor until the test lamp lights. Have several attempts to establish the precise position at which the lamp lights, because this shows that the points have just opened. Retighten the clamp bolt. If it is too difficult to connect your test lamp to the distributor you can attach it to the two coil low-tension terminals, in which case the test lamp will go out when the points open. This method of timing is known as static timing.

Another method is stroboscopic timing, which is done when the engine is running. Some modern cars can only be timed by this method. The stroboscopic timing light is simply a light that flashes on and off when linked into the No. 1 sparking plug circuit. First you must make sure the timing marks are clearly visible, and for the best results you should use a tachometer so the engine revs can be set to the recommended level, usually around 600—800 rev/min. Normally, the timing is done with the vacuum advance disconnected and the carburettor stub pipe plugged, but the handbook will give details. With the engine running, point the light at the timing marks. If the timing is correct, the appropriate mark should appear stationary and in line with the pointer. If it is not, rotate the distributor as before until it is.

You can also check the automatic advance by revving the engine, when the timing mark should seem to move backwards.

No ignition system will run efficiently if proper attention is not paid to the spark plugs. Simple maintenance requirements are that the plugs should be removed at 8000 or 10 000 km (5000 or 6000 miles), cleaned, checked, re-gapped and, if sound, refitted. At 16 000 km (10 000 miles) they should be thrown away and a new set fitted.

Changing them is a simple enough operation. It is important that the order of the leads should not be mixed up. Usually it is easy to place the leads so that their positions are obvious. If there is any chance of mixing them up, mark them by wrapping a ring of masking tape on each and numbering it.

Take the old plugs out using the proper tool. A universal plug spanner will tackle most engines, but one with deeply recessed spark plugs may need a special thin-walled box-type spanner. One with an extended handle might be needed, if there is some other access difficulty. Loosen each plug and wipe away any dirt or rust from the seat before extracting it.

Take great care when fitting new ones to ensure they are not cross threaded. If this happens in an alloy head, it will destroy the thread. Although this is repairable, using a helicoil, it is time-wasting and aggravating.

If the plugs are to be refitted, clean them with a fine wire brush or, better still, have them sandblasted clean at your local garage. Handy for setting the gap is the little gapping tool sold for the job. This combines a lever for setting the earth electrode, feeler gauges for measuring the gap, and a small file for squaring off the electrodes. The recommended plug gap is usually 0.64 mm (0.025 in), but follow the figures given in the car handbook.

Always fit the correct plug for the car — long reach or short reach, normal or extended nose, and, of course, the right heat range. Fit the actual plug recommended if you can, or another manufacturer's direct equivalent if not.

Most of the work possible on the ignition system has been detailed in this chapter. For troubleshooting details turn to the table on pages 130—133.

Routine ignition maintenance is to look after the points and the plugs and, if carbon-thread high-tension leads are used, to change them about every twelve months. Most important of all, keep the whole system clean.

## COLD-START COIL

Quite a lot of modern cars are now fitted with 'cold-start' coils (Figure 6.10). When the starter motor is used, the heavy current demand pulls the battery voltage down seriously, which automatically weakens the spark at the plugs. To avoid

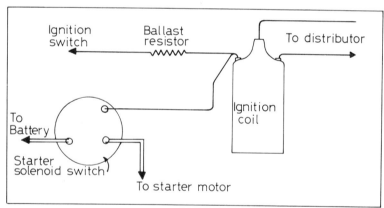

**Figure 6.10** Cold-start (easy-start) coil circuit

this, the cold-start or low-voltage coil (6, 8, or 9 volts depending on the car to which it is fitted) is used, with a series or ballast resistor to reduce battery voltage to that required by the coil.

When the starter motor is operated, an extra contact in the solenoid closes and connects the coil terminal to the main battery circuit so it receives the full battery voltage, reduced by the starter load to the required level, enabling the coil to deliver its full high-tension voltage to the plugs for easy starting.

The resistor is often fitted to the 'live' terminal of the ignition coil or on a small bracket mounted on the engine or bodywork near the coil. In many cases, however, it consists of a length of resistance wire incorporated in the wiring loom.

Never try to use a cold-start coil in the ordinary ignition system, because without the resistor it will be damaged; conversely, you can't use the normal coil in a ballast resistor circuit.

# 7 Lighting

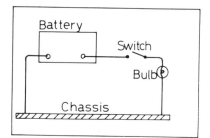

**Figure 7.1** Basic side-light circuit

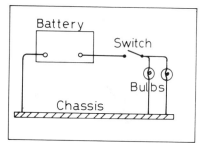

**Figure 7.2** One battery and one switch operate two lamps

In Chapter 1 the basic wiring circuit was explained, as well as the method of testing for faults using a test lamp and leads. We shall now see how the lighting system is built up as an interlocking system of separate basic circuits.

Take side lights first. We have our basic circuit of battery, switch, lamp, and the connecting wires; note that the chassis forms part of the 'wiring' (Figure 7.1). Now instead of *repeating* this circuit for each lamp, we simply *add* to the circuit. So we then have Figure 7.2, where one battery and one switch operate two lamps; by further addition, this becomes the full side and rear light circuit (Figure 7.3).

Using the Lucas system of colour coding (see Chapter 1) the wire from the battery to the switch would be brown and the rest of the circuit red. On some cars the circuit is fused

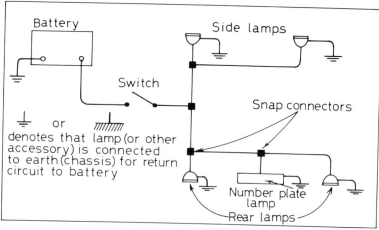

**Figure 7.3** Full side and rear light circuit

for protection against shorts. The fuse may be one of several in a fuse block or, in some cases, a line fuse in the wire from the switch to the first snap-connector junction (Figure 7.4). Note that the colour code changes after the fuse, a coloured trace appearing along the red wire. A further variation occurs on some cars which have the lights fused in pairs: either left-hand lights and right-hand lights, or diagonally (Figure 7.5).

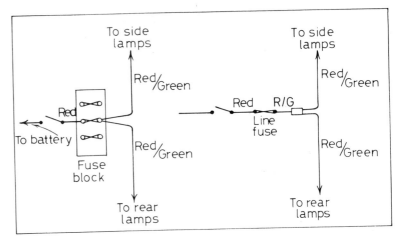

**Figure 7.4** How fuses are incorporated

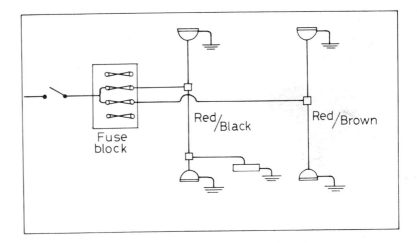

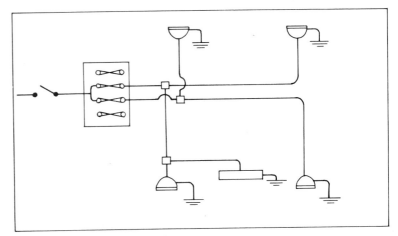

**Figure 7.5** Lights fused in pairs

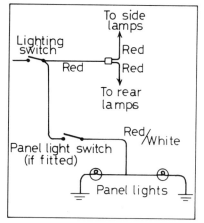

**Figure 7.6** Panel-light wiring

The panel lights are also switched on by the side-light switch, but may have their own switch so that they can be turned off when not required. The colour code for panel-light wiring is red/white (Figure 7.6). The panel-light switch is sometimes in the form of a variable resistance so that the lights can be dimmed to prevent glare.

The headlamps usually have a circuit similar to the side lights, with the addition of a switch to select main or dipped beam. The main switch is incorporated with the side-light switch as one unit. As with side lights, some cars have the headlamp circuit fused (Figure 7.7). Headlamps usually consist of sealed-beam units or bulbs containing two filaments.

## HEADLAMP UNITS

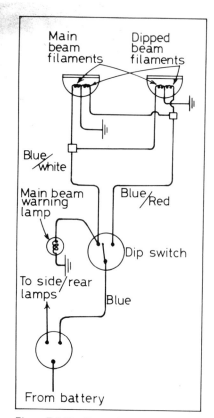

**Figure 7.7** Headlamp circuit

Earlier headlamps used a pre-focused bulb fitted into the back of a specially shaped reflector, which was sealed to a lens designed to focus the beam to give maximum illumination of the road with minimum glare and dazzle to other drivers.

These lamps were later superseded by the sealed-beam unit, which had no separate bulb. The reflector and lens were all in one with the filaments mounted inside; the whole unit was gas filled, making, in effect, one large bulb. They were made in both round and rectangular shapes. However, the latest trend with rectangular units is to revert to the earlier system of reflector and lens with a separate bulb. Electrically there is no difference: wiring and testing are exactly the same for both types.

A further innovation was the introduction of tungsten halogen bulbs. Ordinary bulbs have a filament consisting of a coil of fine tungsten wire. When electric current is passed through the coil, it heats up to such an extent that it becomes incandescent and gives off light. To prevent the tungsten filament from burning away, the air is exhausted from the bulb and replaced by an inert gas. However, particles of tungsten do become detached and settle on the inside of the bulb, blackening the glass and causing loss of light. The sealed-beam unit overcame this to a certain extent because the glass surface is so much greater in area.

Halogen bulbs go under different names — quartz halogen, quartz iodine, tungsten halogen and so on — but they are all the same thing, consisting of a quartz envelope containing a tungsten filament. The quartz can stand up to much more heat than glass, and can therefore be made much more compact. The air inside the envelope is exhausted and then, instead of an inert gas that has no effect on the action of the filament, a small quantity of iodine is introduced (iodine is one of a group of four elements known as halogens, hence the name of the bulb). When the tungsten filament gets hot,

the iodine vaporises and the bulb emits a much brighter light
than the normal filament. Never look directly at one of these
bulbs when it is switched on: it can cause damage to the eyes.

Halogen bulbs can be obtained to replace most types of
conventional headlamp, spot and fog light bulbs. Never hold
the quartz envelope of a halogen bulb with the bare fingers,
since normal skin moisture can damage it. Hold it by the
metal part or with a clean dry cloth.

## FLASHER UNIT

Flashing direction indicators are operated by a small sealed
unit, either a cylindrical capsule with three terminals (Lucas
FL5), or a little rectangular unit (Lucas 8FL), which is the
later type and has two terminals. Figure 7.8 shows a typical
circuit for each type of unit.

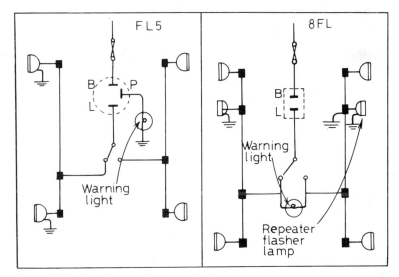

**Figure 7.8** Typical direction-indicator circuits

## BULB REPLACEMENT

Bulb replacement in the smaller lamps — side, rear, indicator,
and so forth — is straightforward. Where the lens is secured
by screws through a bezel, after the screws have been removed
the bezel can be lifted away followed by the lens, taking care
not to damage the damp-excluding rubber backing. Some
circular lenses are held in place by a chrome rim and rubber
lip, so you use a small screwdriver to prise the lens free. When
replacing the lens, a smear of washing-up liquid on the rubber
helps to get the lens back into place. Some rear lamps have
the bulb holders held to the lamp bodies by spring clips. To
remove these you simply pull the lamp holders out of the lamp
bodies. Replace the bulb holders carefully and squarely so
that the spring tabs are not damaged; if there is a locating slot,
see that it engages properly, otherwise the holder will not go in.

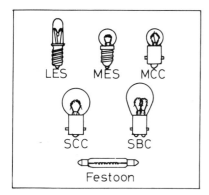

**Figure 7.9** Types of small bulb commonly used in cars

Some Ford rear lamps have a plastic bulb holder with a small metal strip to act as an earth, running in a groove on the side. Replacing a bulb in this type of holder must be done very carefully as it is possible to push the strip up through the holder until it pops out of the top. It could then touch the lamp contacts, causing a short and blowing the fuse when the lights are switched on.

Bulbs are rated in watts, i.e. the power consumed by the bulb. As a point of interest, the wattage is the product of the circuit voltage and the current consumed. In a 12-volt circuit a 36-watt bulb would consume three amps, a 6-watt bulb would consume half an amp, and so on.

Always make sure you replace dud bulbs with the correct type. There are different sizes and types of caps, and the wrong bulb can give rise to troubles. A selection is shown in Figure 7.9.

Bulb caps come in several sizes and they all have names formed from initials which can be confusing. Tiny screw-in bulbs are known as LES (Lilliput Edison Screw); bigger screw-in types (flash-lamp size) are MES (Miniature Edison Screw); small bayonet bulbs are MCC (Miniature Centre Contact). More common is the SCC (Small Centre Contact), which is a single-filament bulb in various wattages, used for some side lights, rear lamps, direction indicators and similar applications. The double-filament type in this size is the SBC (Small Bayonet Cap); its locating pins are either directly opposite each other or, more commonly, offset ('indexed'). Indexed pins ensure that the bulb can only be inserted the right way round, since the two filaments are of different wattages. Stop/rear bulbs usually have a six-watt filament for the rear light and a 21-watt filament for the stop light.

A recent innovation is the wedge-base or capless bulb in various small sizes for instrument lighting, side, and number-plate lights. This type, as its name implies, has no metal cap, just two small pieces of wire protruding from the glass envelope and bent round the wedge-shaped base to make contact with the contacts in the bulb holder.

One other type in fairly common usage is the festoon bulb. Usually used in interior (roof) lights, it is a tubular bulb with a conical cap at either end. It is also used on some continental cars for side lights and flashing indicators.

Headlamp bulb replacement is not quite so simple because it often means removing the whole unit, although on some cars you can remove the bulb from inside the bonnet. On a majority of vehicles however, it means removing the headlamp bezel (older models are secured by a screw in the underside and a clip at the top), or even the complete front grille. With the rim or grille removed, the inner rim (secured by small self-tapping screws) can be taken out. Some reflector units have three spring-loaded screws through the body of the reflector: by pressing inwards and twisting anti-clockwise, the unit can be freed, allowing access to the bulb holder at the rear. Some units with separate bulbs have the bulb held by wire clips.

## HEADLAMP ALIGNMENT

Headlamps must be aligned to prevent dazzle to other motorists. The old method of facing the car against a wall or garage door for beam adjustment is not satisfactory with modern, high-powered lights, and should not be attempted except as a temporary measure. If you must, the method is to point the car head-on at a blank wall from 8 metres (25 feet) away and to make chalk crosses at the same distance apart as the lamp centres, the horizontal line being slightly lower than the height of the lamp centres from the ground. The lamp main beams are then set until the centre of the beam is aligned on the chalk cross.

There are three adjusting screws for each lamp, one on either side and one at the top. Adjust the beam with the two side screws to align the beam with the vertical line of the cross, screwing one in and the other out by equal amounts. When the horizontal alignment is satisfactory, adjust the beam vertically using the top screw. This really is only a temporary method, and the proper way is to have the beams set by a garage with a beam setter. It will not cost a great deal.

Remember, if you are carrying unusually heavy loads at the rear (say holiday luggage in the boot plus two extra rear-seat passengers) that your beam level will be higher and may well dazzle other drivers, even on dipped lights.

## COMMON FAULTS

Faults likely to occur in lighting circuits, other than the expected one of bulbs failing in service, are short circuits and faulty connections. 'Shorts' are chiefly caused by wires chafing on sharp metal edges where the wires run through the car's body.

With a short, what happens is that the electric current can run from the battery, through the switch (when on), and then takes the path of least resistance to earth (Figure 7.10) instead of passing through the lamp. Without the natural resistance of the lamp to control the current flow, an excessive current flows in this part of the circuit. If the circuit is fused, the high current will cause the fuse wire to melt, breaking the circuit like a switch, and preventing damage. In an unfused circuit, however, there is no such protection; instead of the fuse wire melting, the wiring of the circuit will get very hot. This can cause the insulation to melt along its length so that the wire itself is exposed. There is then a risk of further short circuits, and the whole section of the wiring harness involved can catch fire.

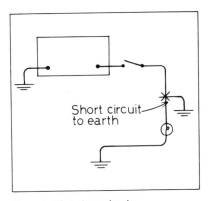

**Figure 7.10** A short-circuit

This in itself is not usually very serious, apart from local damage to the wiring. The insulation does not burn fiercely and the affected wire generally burns through and breaks the circuit in the same manner as a fuse blowing. But if there is any petrol or petrol vapour about, matters could become very serious. It is therefore as well to check the wiring from time to time to spot any chafing before it gets to the critical stage. Places to watch are where cables pass through holes in metal panels (these points should always be fitted with rubber grommets to protect the cables) and at metal clips that secure cables to the car body, especially those where the cables run across the front of the car below the radiator grille (Leyland) and under the engine (Vauxhall).

Another cause of short circuits is snap connectors used to join two or more cables, where the cable ends are not pressed fully home into the rubber sleeves. The protruding bit of metal may touch the car body and cause a short, particularly in the boot close to the rear-lamp clusters.

Other causes of lamp failure are bad connections due to loose terminals at switches and similar places, and corrosion in snap connectors. Push-on terminals can be squeezed gently with a small pair of pliers, nuts and screws can be tightened, and snap connectors can be separated (if you are lucky!) and scraped clean — although it is better to replace them with new ones.

Corrosion can also cause trouble in the lamps themselves. Again, scraping the corroded connectors can very often effect a cure, but if the corrosion is very bad replacement is the only answer. Don't forget that the actual point of bad corrosion may be on the *earth* side of the lamp. On the *live* side the fault can be between the wire terminal and the lamp contact, or between the lamp contact and the bulb; on the *earth* side it can be between bulb and bulb holder, between bulb holder and lamp body, or between lamp body and car body (Figure 7.11). This applies to all lamps on the car.

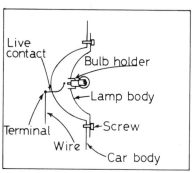

Figure 7.11 Where corrosion can cause poor electrical contact on a lamp

## FAULT-FINDING ROUTINES

Although lighting and indicator circuits may appear complicated, it is not really so if you remember the basic circuit. In fact, most faults almost locate themselves.

### Side and rear lights

Suppose the rear lamps are not working when the lights are switched on. If the side and panel lights work, the fault cannot be in the feed to the switch or the switch itself — a simple, logical deduction. Hence that section of the circuit does not need to be tested. Check the fuses, since some cars have the rear lamps fused separately. *If the fuse has blown* replace it; if the lights come on and stay on, it may just have been a faulty fuse. However, check the rear lamp wiring for chafed wires or a bullet (snap) connector not pushed fully home, especially in the boot.

*If the fuse blows again immediately*, disconnect the rear-lamp wiring in the boot, either at the bullet connectors (if any) or from the lamps, not forgetting the number-plate light. Now, with the rear lamps disconnected, replace the fuse. *If it blows yet again*, the fault must lie between the fuse box and the point where you disconnected the lamps; this means that at some point the wire has become damaged, perhaps by chafing on a sharp metal edge, under the carpet, or behind a trim panel. If any welding has been done to the body recently, the heat could have damaged the wiring on the other side of a panel, which often happens. You will simply have to examine the wiring until you find the fault.

*If the fuse does not blow with the rear lamps disconnected*, reconnect the lamps one by one until you find the one that blows the fuse, and then examine the lamp to find the cause. It may be a bent contact that is touching the lamp body, or even a faulty bulb. A fault that can occur if any repair work has been carried out is that the lamps have been connected wrongly, with the live wire going to the earth terminal. Another common fault is loose gear in the boot — tools, petrol can, folding pram, golf trolley — touching lamp terminals.

*If there is no fuse* for the rear lamps, there must be a different kind of fault (an *open* circuit, whereas the previous one was a short circuit) and the test procedure is rather different. Of course it *could* be just a couple of dud bulbs, so check them first.

If the bulbs are all right, take out your test lamp and connect one terminal to earth and the other to a known live point to check that the test lamp is working properly; check it at frequent intervals to make sure it continues to work.

It doesn't matter which end of the circuit you start from, but usually (simply because of the way instrument panels on modern cars are boxed in) it is easier to start at the lamp end. We know that in this case the switch is all right because the front lights are working, so check for current with the test lamp at the snap connector where the lamp wires join the main wiring (Figure 7.12). If the lamp does not light, the fault must be between this point and the switch. The wire

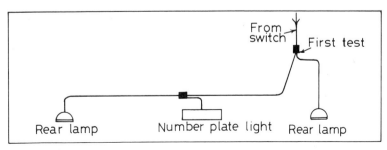

**Figure 7.12** Test points in a rear-lamp circuit

D

may have come away from the switch, or if there is a snap connector where the switch wire and the wires to the lamp join there could be a faulty connection. You will usually find this point where the wires running to the back join the main wiring behind the instrument panel, just above the trim panel in front of the left or right front door. Sometimes the snap connectors are tucked behind the trim panels, although on Minis the junction is under the bonnet just above the screen-washer bottle. If your test lamp shows there is current here, it means that the wire is damaged somewhere between front and rear; you will have to remove trim panels and inspect the cables. Welding repairs are often responsible for this type of fault.

There may be no snap connector in the boot, as some cars have the junction made at one of the lamp terminals (Figure 7.13), so check that there is a good connection. Use your test lamp to see if there is current: if the lamp lights the fault must be in the lamps themselves, usually due to corrosion in the lamps or between the lamps and the car body. Of course, if only one lamp does not light you won't have to check the wiring from the switch: the other lamp will have done that for you!

If the rear lamp lights but not the side lamps, the same test procedure applies.

If neither side nor rear lamps light when switched on, first check the fuse if one is fitted. Where there is no fuse start checking at the switch. See if there is a 'live' feed by connecting

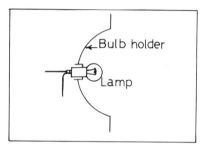

**Figure 7.13** Junction point on a lamp terminal

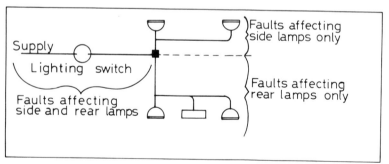

**Figure 7.14** Faults localised to one section of a circuit

the test lamp between the brown-wire terminal and earth. If this is all right, check the output terminal (red wire); no current here means the switch is faulty. Should the test lamp light, move to the main snap connector junction and check as previously described; the fault cannot be beyond here as this is as far as the common circuit to front and rear goes.

So you see that all these types of fault can be localised to one section of the circuit (Figure 7.14).

## Headlamps

The headlamp circuit can also be broken down into sections for testing, except that there is an extra switch, the dip switch (Figure 7.15). When neither dipped nor main-beam lamps work, the fault is most likely to be the main lighting switch or the dip switch. Use the test lamp at input and output terminals of both switches to find which one is faulty.

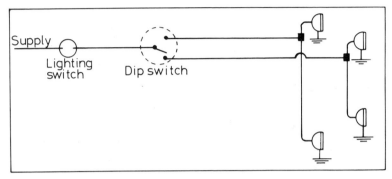

**Figure 7.15** Headlamp circuit incorporates a dip switch

## Direction indicators

The direction-indicator circuit can also be broken down into sections for testing, but with additional units to check (Figure 7.8).

A fault can often be located by a quick study of the symptoms. For instance, if the indicators operate correctly on one side, a fault in the supply (fuse or flasher unit) can be ruled out as these are common to both sides. In such a case, the logical point to start is at the indicator switch. A check with the test lamp — one terminal earthed — will show whether there is current at the output switch terminal on the faulty side; if there is none, the switch itself is dud. It is very easy, when wiring work has been carried out, to get the green/red and green/brown switch wires crossed over, so check the connections to the switch.

If you get a positive result at this point, move on to the snap connector where the wires to front and rear branch off.

When the indicators do not operate at all, the fault could be the fuse, the flasher unit, or the switch. On steering-column switches it is not unusual for the feed wire (green/brown) to break away from the terminal. Also switch contacts often get deformed, and a little judicious bending with a small pair of pointed-nose pliers can often get the switch working again.

Indicators that light but do not flash, or that flash very slowly, can usually be blamed on a lazy flasher unit if it is one of the Lucas 8FL rectangular pattern. Slow flashing will also occur with the 8FL unit if one or more of the indicator bulbs has a lower wattage than normal; this can be caused by bulb deterioration or corrosion preventing the full current from passing. The corrosion may be between the lamp and car body, in the lamp unit, or in the bulb holder.

Very fast flashing, with the 8FL unit, is caused by a faulty flasher unit or by overloading due to a partial short circuit. Test by joining the two wires to the flasher unit and operating the switch: the lamps should light up but not flash.

On circuits using the cylindrical type of flasher unit (Lucas FL5), the symptoms are reversed: overloading slows the rate of flashing, but a reduced load (such as a faulty bulb) speeds it up.

It is possible to replace the small 8FL flasher unit with the FL5 cylindrical type (which is more reliable and less sensitive) by transferring the B and L wires from one unit to the other and disregarding the P terminal on the FL5 unit. If the wires are fitted into a socket that pushes on to the 8FL flasher-unit terminals, you will have to pull the tags out of the terminal block first, as the location of the terminals on the FL5 unit is different.

# 8 Instruments

Instrumentation can vary tremendously, ranging from two simple dials and two warning lights to something that looks like the instrument panel of an airliner. The instrument common to all cars is the speedometer, but that's usually mechanical anyway, except for the illumination light. Everything else, however, is electrical: the range includes rev counter (tachometer), petrol gauge, temperature gauge, battery-condition indicator (voltmeter), ammeter, and the various warning lights.

## REV COUNTERS

There are four types: cable-driven, a.c. voltmeter, electronic current-impulse and voltage-triggered.

As its name suggests, the *cable-driven* type is not electrical but is operated mechanically in the same way as a speedometer.

The *a.c. voltmeter* type is really just an a.c. voltmeter that is scaled in rev/min instead of volts. It is energised by a small a.c. generator, driven off the end of the camshaft on some earlier cars. If it stops working, a check can be made by connecting a small 6-volt bulb across the generator output terminals. If the bulb lights when the engine is revved, the generator is sound and the fault is in the instrument. If it does not light, the fault is in the generator and this will have to be renewed.

This type of rev counter, often fitted to Jaguars, can only be operated in conjunction with its proper generator, so don't buy one from the local breaker's yard and fit it to your Mini because you like the look of it; you'd have to fit the Jaguar engine as well to work it!

*Electronic current-impulse* types are transistorised instruments. They are usually polarised, i.e. they have to be matched to the polarity of the battery connections, either positive earth or negative earth. Thus the positive-earth and negative-earth types are not interchangeable; universal types are available, however, with a terminal arrangement that allows connection to systems of either polarity. The impulse section of the instrument is connected in such a way that the current impulses in the ignition circuit, as the distributor contacts open and close, pass through the instrument and are converted into magnetic impulses, which pull the needle around the scale.

Since the instrument is transistorised, if faulty it should be returned to the manufacturer or an instrument specialist for repair. There are few checks possible on a DIY basis. If the engine is running there is nothing basically wrong with the ignition circuit, and that leaves only the connections to the instrument. Check first that the relevant contact becomes live when the ignition is switched on, and then that the instrument case is earthed properly.

The *voltage-triggered* tachometer is essentially a transistorised voltmeter, which measures the frequency of the volt drop across the ignition coil as the distributor contacts open and close. Again, fault finding is limited to checking that the wiring between ignition coil and instrument is in order. Any fault in the instrument itself is a job for the specialist.

**Fitting**

The rev counter is a favourite instrument for the DIY man to fit as an extra. If the instrument is bought new, there is seldom any problem because it comes complete with instructions. Problems usually arise when someone purchases the dial secondhand and then tries to find out how to wire it. It's not necessarily a difficult job, but it does vary from make to make. As an example, Figure 8.1 shows the connections required for three popular makes — Yazaki, Smiths and Veglia Borletti. The siting and fitting of the dial are described at the end of this chapter.

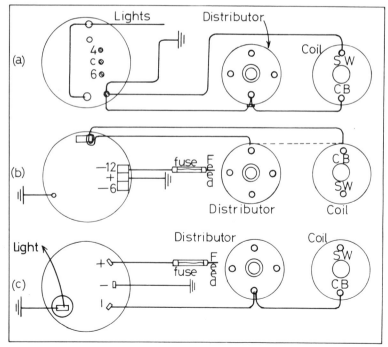

**Figure 8.1** Connections for various makes of tachometer: (a) Yazaki, (b) Smiths, (c) Veglia-Borletti

## FUEL, WATER-TEMPERATURE AND OIL-PRESSURE GAUGES

These three are essentially the same instrument. In fact, for fault finding, the instrument connections can be changed over to compare results.

### Dynamometer type

The older type dynamometer type has two opposing windings acting on the needle magnet (Figure 8.2). When the ignition is switched on, current is fed to one end of both coils. The other end of one coil (control winding) is connected to earth; the current flowing through this coil sets up a magnetic field, which acts on the small magnet fixed to the needle. In the case of a fuel gauge, if no current were flowing in the other coil, the needle would be pulled over to the FULL position.

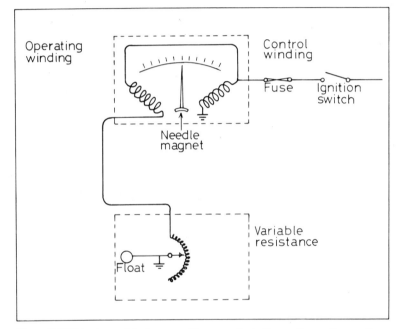

**Figure 8.2** Older type of fuel gauge with opposed windings acting on the needle magnet

The other end of the second coil (operating winding) is connected to a resistance in the tank unit of the system. In the tank unit, a float on the end of a stiff wire arm, pivoted in the body of the unit, moves a collector contact over the resistance as the float moves up and down with the level of fuel in the tank. The variation of resistance in the circuit of the operating coil causes a corresponding varying current to flow through the coil; the current is strongest when the float is in the low (empty) position, and weakest when the float is high (full) and all the resistance is in the circuit.

The current flowing in the operating winding sets up an opposing magnetic field in the instrument and pulls the needle towards the EMPTY mark on the scale. The amount of pull depends on the current flow through the winding, which in turn depends on the amount of fuel in the tank.

Testing, with this type of instrument, is fairly simple. *If no reading is obtained when the ignition is on* (assuming, of course, that the tank is not indeed empty), disconnect the wire from the tank unit. The meter should now read FULL. If it does, the fault is in the tank unit, which must be removed for inspection.

The most likely fault here is a punctured float that has filled with petrol and sunk. A metal float can be repaired as follows. Boil up a saucepan of water and remove it from the flame. Immerse the float in the boiling water to evaporate the petrol from it. Do this well away from any naked lights — the vapour given off is highly explosive. Repeat this operation until the float is empty and all the fumes have been driven off, and then carefully solder over the hole.

If the float is plastic, a hole can be sealed with plastic cement, provided it is not soluble in petrol. Generally, however, it is better to replace a defective plastic unit with either a new one or a secondhand one obtained from a breaker's yard.

If the meter still shows EMPTY when the tank-unit wire is disconnected, remove the wire from the T terminal of the instrument. If the meter now reads FULL, the fault is a short circuit to earth of the wire between instrument and tank unit. If the dial still shows EMPTY, the instrument is at fault.

*If the dial wrongly shows FULL when the ignition is switched on,* remove the tank-unit wire and connect to earth. The instrument should read EMPTY. If it does, there is an open circuit in the tank unit: either the resistance wire is broken or disconnected from the terminal, or the contact fingers are not connecting properly with the resistance.

If the instrument still shows FULL when the tank-unit wire is earthed, connect the T terminal of the instrument to earth. An EMPTY reading now means a break or bad connection in the wire from instrument to tank. A FULL reading denotes a faulty instrument.

The temperature and oil-pressure gauges operate in a similar manner, except that the transmitter units are sealed.

As these older types of instrument have their two opposing windings supplied from the same source, readings are not affected by minor voltage variations in the system. Voltage does vary because, when the car is running, with lights being switched on and off and the charge rate varying with engine speed, the battery voltage can be anything from about 11 volts to 15 volts at any given time.

The readings on this type of gauge are immediate. In the case of fuel gauges, the older cars to which they are fitted have the problem of needle variation due to fuel surge in the tank, even though baffles are fitted to minimise it. Steep hills and steep road cambers can also affect the readings slightly, so the only time a true reading is given is when the car is travelling steadily on a straight and level road. You can tell if you have one of these gauges fitted, because the needle flicks over the scale to give a reading immediately the ignition is switched on.

**Thermal type**

The instrument that has now almost universally replaced the dynamometer type operates on the thermal principle of expansion or contraction of a wire when a small current is passed through it.

It works as a result of the variation of current flowing through the operating wire. This, in turn, is determined by the variation of the resistance of the transmitter unit, whether caused by the fuel level, water or oil temperature, oil pressure or whatever.

Any voltage variation in the system will affect the readings, so a controlled voltage is necessary. To achieve this, the instruments operate on a lower voltage than the main circuits (either 8 or 10 volts); this is supplied by a small unit known as the *instrument voltage stabiliser* (IVS), a thermally controlled unit that sends pulses of current to the instruments, with an average voltage equal to that required by the particular instrument system in use.

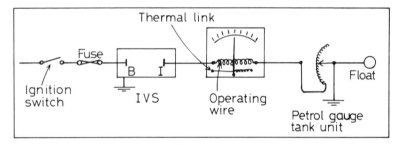

**Figure 8.3** Fuel gauge circuit using IVS

Instrument operation is simple (Figure 8.3). When the ignition is switched on and the system energised, the current from the IVS passes through the operating wire of the instrument to the transmitter unit, and through the variable resistance of the transmitter to earth to complete the circuit.

Current passing through the operating wire of the instrument causes it to get warm and expand, allowing the spring tension in the needle linkage to pull the needle over the scale to give the required reading. As the resistance of the transmitter varies (whether due to movement of the fuel-gauge float moving the contact finger over the resistance in the tank unit, or due to the effect of varying temperature or pressure on the engine transmitters), so the current flowing in the operating wire of the instrument will vary. This, in turn, causes the wire to heat up or cool down and, balanced by the spring tension, move the needle across the scale.

There is a time lag while the operating wire warms up or cools, so when the ignition is switched on the needle creeps slowly across the dial. When the engine is running, of course, this time lag does not matter: the change of resistance occurs only slowly as the fuel level goes down or the engine warms up, etc. It is a positive advantage, since fuel surge will not affect the needle.

Fault finding is simple if you work to a system. Usually there are at least two instruments operating through the IVS: fuel gauge and water temperature gauge. If both gauges read consistently high or low, the IVS is obviously suspect, since it is the only thing they have in common.

*If both gauges fail to read at all*, check the supply to the IVS. On most cars this is fitted behind the speedometer, but there are a few models where it is on the bulkhead, either inside the car or in the engine compartment. If current is definitely being supplied, check the IVS output terminal; if this is faulty it must be renewed. Use a very small test lamp for this check — a 12-volt, 2.2-watt panel-light bulb is suitable.

*If both gauges go off the scale at the top end*, there's either a fault in the IVS itself or its earth connection is faulty or has come adrift. It is a good idea to run a separate wire from the screw that secures the IVS to the speedometer to a suitable earth point on the car body. This is because the IVS often depends for its earth on the earth connection of the speedometer illumination light, and this can be making poor contact at the speedometer end.

*If only one gauge is not operating correctly*, while the other one is working normally, the fault is not connected with the IVS. The procedure for locating it is the same for all the similarly designed instruments. If there is no reading at all, remove the wire from the transmitter terminal and connect to earth. Switch the ignition on and watch the needle. If it starts to move across the dial, switch off the ignition; *don't* let the needle go right over. If the needle moves, the circuit through the instrument to the transmitter is in order and the fault must be in the transmitter itself. Usually a replacement is required, but in the case of the fuel gauge it may be that the float is punctured and has sunk, or there is no earth connection between the fuel tank and chassis.

If there is no movement of the needle in the above test, earth the transmitter terminal of the instrument. If the needle then moves when the ignition is switched on, the fault is in the wire from instrument to transmitter. If there is still no movement, suspect the instrument itself.

Since these instruments are identical internally, only the markings on the dials being different, a simple check is to change the wires from one instrument to another. Don't worry that the terminals aren't marked. The heating up of the operating wire will be the same whichever way they are connected.

If you wish, it is simple to distinguish the wires, however. Cables from the IVS to the instruments will all be light green with a blue trace or plain light green. Wires to the transmitter will be green/black on the fuel gauge, green/blue on the temperature gauge.

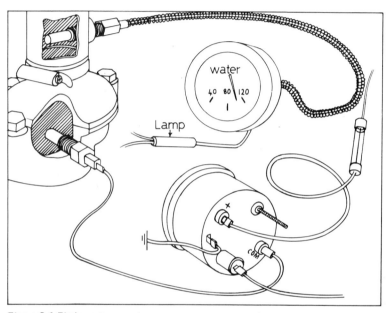

**Figure 8.4** Fitting a temperature or pressure gauge

## Fitting

If there is no water-temperature or oil-pressure gauge, these can be purchased and added quite easily (see Figure 8.4).

Fitting the electrical type of gauge involves two mechanical jobs. First the transmitter has to be screwed into the appropriate tapping in the block or in the head. Usually it's simply a matter of removing a plug or the existing oil-pressure switch and screwing the transmitter in its place. Second, the dial has to be mounted in the dash panel: see the end of the chapter.

From the back of the dial there are three wiring connections. One goes to the transmitter, via a grommetted hole in the bulkhead. The second is linked to an ignition-controlled power source, probably the accessories terminal on either the ignition switch or the fusebox. The third is linked, using a snap connector, into the panel-illumination circuit.

There is another type of water-temperature gauge where the dial and transmitter are linked by a capillary tube. The only electrical connection to this type is to link in the dial illumination bulb.

## BATTERY-CONDITION INDICATOR

The battery-condition indicator is really a voltmeter, and is similar to the petrol-gauge type instruments. However, since it has to show the actual voltage of the battery it is not supplied through the IVS. The indicator is usually connected between the ignition switch or ignition-controlled fuse and earth, so that the current flowing through the operating wire will vary with battery voltage.

When the ignition is switched on, the needle will creep up to read about 12 volts, which is the nominal battery voltage when standing. A reading below this denotes that the battery is not fully charged. If it is well down (and provided nothing has been left on accidentally), it probably means that the battery will not hold its charge when left standing.

When the engine is started and the generator begins to charge the battery, the needle will creep up the scale, finally reaching a reading between 13.5 and 14.5 volts. At 2500 rev/min the reading should remain steady between these figures when headlamps, wipers and heater blower are all switched on.

If the needle starts to creep downwards, for some reason the charging system is not coping with the load; probably the fan belt is slipping or the control box needs adjusting.

If the needle reads more than 15 volts (usually a red sector) the battery is being overcharged or is faulty. To avoid serious damage to the generator and/or the battery, the system should be checked immediately.

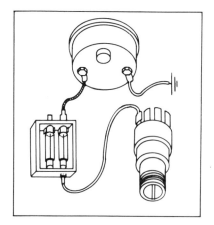

**Figure 8.5** Fitting a battery-condition indicator

### Fitting

Wiring a battery-condition indicator as an extra is straight-forward (see Figure 8.5). The connections have already been mentioned: one goes to the switch side of the ignition or the fuse carrier and the other to earth.

## AMMETER

While the battery-condition indicator shows the actual voltage across the battery, the ammeter indicates current flowing into or out of the battery, or the difference (algebraic sum) of the two.

For instance, if lights etc. are switched on when the engine is not running, the ammeter will register the actual current being consumed, shown as a discharge or a negative reading.

If the generator is charging with no load switched on, the charge rate will be shown as a charge or positive reading. If the lights are now switched on, the ammeter will show the difference between the two readings. For example, if the generator is charging at 10 amps and the load switched on is 8 amps, the ammeter will register a charge of $10 - 8 = 2$ amps. If, however, another load is switched on, say 5 amps, the ammeter will show $10 - 8 - 5 = -3$ amps (discharge).

The advantage of the ammeter is that it can be used to show exactly how the charging system is working. It also shows instantly whether the charging current is balancing the load. If it isn't, it is usually possible to reduce the load to prevent the battery being run down. The battery-condition indicator will not register an excessive load for some time, nor will it show overcharging, so danger point may well be reached before any indication is given. The ammeter, on the other hand, gives an immediate indication. Ideally the two instruments should be used together.

**Fitting**

Fitting an ammeter to a car where one was not provided as original equipment is not quite as simple as with a battery-condition indicator. Refer to Figure 8.6, where (a), (b) and (c) relate to cars currently in production.

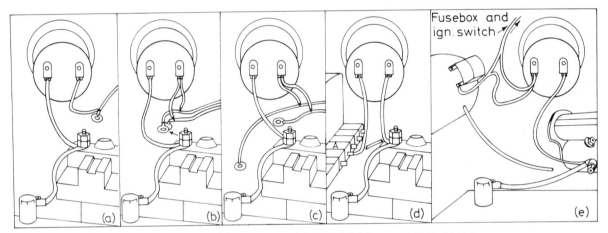

**Figure 8.6** Fitting ammeters: (a) single feed, (b) double feed, (c) split feed, (d) two-coil CVC, (e) Volkswagen

If there is a single plain brown wire leading off from the solenoid main terminal, disconnect it and fit instead one lead to the ammeter. Join the disconnected brown wire to the other ammeter lead. This is the system at (a).

In the system shown at (b) there is more than one wire joined to the solenoid. Disconnect all of these, twist them together, join in one of the ammeter leads and solder the connection. Join the second ammeter lead to the now vacant connection point on the solenoid.

The split-feed system shown at (c) is the same as (b), except for that battery-connected wire. Disconnect all the wires from both battery and solenoid. Join them together along with one ammeter lead. Connect the other ammeter wire either to the battery or the solenoid.

The wiring you might well see on an older car is shown at (d). It's the same as (a) except that the brown wire should be disconnected completely; one ammeter wire goes to the solenoid and the other to A on the two-bobbin control box.

Wiring an ammeter into a Volkswagen is tackled a little differently, mainly to save wiring as the dash panel and engine are a long way apart. Remove first the wire between the starter and the junction point on the dynamo. Disconnect the ignition end of the wire between the dynamo junction and the ignition switch, and connect it to the ammeter. Run a new wire from the ammeter through the car to the starter, and add a new wire from the ignition switch to the ammeter to provide return power.

In cases of doubt there is one method of fitting that will suit all cases. Remove the thinner wire(s) from the 'live' terminal of the starter solenoid switch and/or battery, and extend with the appropriate size of cable to one ammeter terminal. Connect the other ammeter terminal to either the starter solenoid or the battery terminal.

After fitting, test the ammeter by switching on the ignition and the headlights. If a charge is shown instead of a discharge, reverse the connections on the back. Ensure that you use the correct wire for the ammeter: it should be 44/0.30 mm (44/0.012 in) when a dynamo is used, 65/0.30 mm (65/0.012 in) for an alternator system.

## WARNING LIGHTS

These are usually incorporated in the instrument panel, either in addition to or instead of some instruments, or simply to show that certain circuits are switched on. Some are legal requirements: warning lights must be wired in circuit with a manually switched reverse light and in circuit with flashing indicators. Another that is likely to be found is a headlamp main-beam warning lamp. The circuit for each of these three is simple: just a wire taken from the circuit concerned to one warning-bulb terminal. The other bulb terminal is usually connected to the common instrument-panel earth.

The oil-pressure warning light (usually amber) and ignition warning light (red) each have one terminal connected to the ignition switch or ignition-controlled fuse. The other terminal of the oil warning light is connected to the oil-pressure switch; this opens, putting the warning light out, when pressure builds up. The other terminal of the ignition warning light is connected to the output terminal of the generator (or a special terminal in the alternator), which becomes live when the generator is charging.

When the ignition is switched on, the light terminal connected to the ignition switch becomes 'live', current flows through the bulb to the generator and through the windings to earth, and the bulb lights. When the generator starts to charge, a voltage equal to that of the battery builds up on the generator terminal of the warning light. With both light terminals at the same voltage, no current can flow through the bulb, which goes out.

When the engine is switched off, the generator is still charging so there will be a temporary current flow and the bulb will light up for a few seconds. If the wrong bulb (too big) is fitted, it may even pass sufficient current to keep the engine running.

If the bulb stays alight when the engine is at rest, on dynamo systems it means the cut-out contacts have failed to separate. Rectify this immediately, or the dynamo, control box and even wiring could be burnt out. On alternator systems, it means the regulator unit has developed a fault; although no serious damage should ensue, the fault should be rectified as it will affect alternator output.

Choke warning lights and handbrake warning lights are connected in a similar manner to the oil-pressure light, with one bulb terminal connected to the ignition switch and the other earthed through a switch incorporated in the choke control or handbrake mechanism. Sometimes the choke warning light has a thermal switch in the circuit so that the light only comes on if the choke is left out after the engine has warmed up to operating temperature.

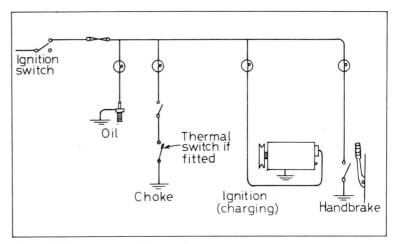

**Figure 8.7** Testing warning-light circuits

Testing any of these circuits (Figure 8.7) is relatively simple. (In the case of indicator and headlamp main-beam warning lights, remember that failure can be due to faulty indicator or headlamp bulbs or bad earth connections.)

To check warning lights that are controlled through the ignition switch, simply disconnect at the terminal of the unit to which they are connected and earth the end of the wire. If the bulb does not light, the chances are that it has failed. The ignition warning light is connected to the dynamo output terminal (either at the dynamo itself or at the D or WL terminal of the control box) by means of a thin brown/yellow wire. In the case of ACR alternators, the brown/yellow wire is connected to the small alternator terminal.

On older cars all the bulbs and instruments have separate wires to them, which makes fault-finding relatively simple, provided you know the wiring colours (see Chapter 1 and page 134).

Later cars have printed-circuit instrument panels, which can cause complications. The idea of these is to make initial assembly easier, and connection to the main wiring is by a multi-way plug and socket. The wires to the plug are coloured in the usual way, but connection from the socket to the various gauges, lamps, etc. is by means of very thin foil links; these are 'printed' on the surface of either the instrument board itself or a plastic sheet, which is secured by small plastic studs to the back of the instrument panel.

Many failures of instruments and lights are caused by faulty plug and socket connections. Make sure that the wiring tags are pushed well home into the back of the plug and that the contact fingers of the plug make a good connection with the contacts of the printed circuit in the socket section. Check also that the plug itself is pushed well home so that it clips into place firmly.

Failure of a bulb to light can obviously be due to failure of the bulb itself. Wedge-base or capless bulbs are usually used, and these sometimes fail to make proper contact if the bulb-holder contacts are corroded or distorted. Another possibility is that the contacts on the bulb holder fail to contact the tags in the bulb-holder sockets of the printed circuit. These sometimes get folded back so that they do not connect when the holder is pushed into place.

Always be very careful when working on a printed circuit: the thin contact strips will burn out like a fuse at the slightest suspicion of a short circuit or overload. Always use a *small* test lamp (with a 12-volt, 2.2-watt panel-light bulb) when checking the continuity of printed circuits.

A damaged contact strip can often be repaired by carefully soldering a short length of 5-amp fuse wire across the break, but if it is badly damaged a new printed circuit will have to be fitted. This is straightforward but handle the circuit board gently and ensure that any faults are rectified before the new unit is fitted, otherwise the new printed circuit will 'blow' as soon as it is switched on.

Bulb replacement on earlier types of instrument panel simply means pulling the bulb holder out of the instrument casing and then unscrewing or unplugging the bulb according to type. Replace with the correct 12-volt 2.2-watt MES or MCC bulb and then refit the bulb holder, taking care to insert it squarely in the hole so that the small spring tongues are not distorted.

Access to these bulbs is often by feeling up from under the dash panel. Sometimes it is a matter of taking out a bayonet-fitting instrument, or perhaps removing part of the dash panel. The handbook or workshop manual for the model concerned is the best guide.

## MOUNTING EXTRA INSTRUMENTS

The fitting of extra instruments is a subject that has recurred throughout this chapter. The wiring of the various types has been covered but it is, of course, necessary also to mount the dials. The modern car's interior design often does not lend itself to additions, and sometimes it is not just a matter of fitting a supplementary instrument panel.

This is obviously the easiest expedient. Supplementary panels can be purchased, attractively finished in chrome or black crackle enamel, with the holes for the instruments already cut. Provided there is a suitable mounting point, it is merely a matter of using the mounting flange and drilling upwards into the underside of the dash for the mounting screws.

An alternative to this is to use the pod-type instrument housing that can be mounted on top of the dash. As the name suggests, this completely shrouds the back of the instrument, leaving only the dial showing. Pods are available for a single instrument or for a 'cluster' if required.

If neither of these alternatives appeals, there is a further possibility, that of purchasing a special console to fit in the area of the gearchange lever. This can be an attractive and useful way of mounting instruments, and often the console will house the radio and cassette player as well.

Occasionally it is possible to mount instruments in the existing dash panel by cutting holes. The best way to do this in a metal panel is to use a fly-cutter or perhaps a hole saw (see Chapter 11). In a wooden dash panel it is a matter of scribing the hole first and then drilling a circle of small inter-locking holes just inside the scribed line. The hole is then finished with a half-round file. It's a time-consuming and tedious method, however.

# 9 Wipers and other accessories

**WINDSCREEN WIPERS**

Two main types of windscreen wiper motor are used: wound field and permanent magnet. The latter is used almost universally on later cars. See Figure 9.1.

**Wound-field motor**

The wound-field motor is a normal shunt-wound motor, with a field coil fitted into the motor body. This generates a magnetic field in which the armature rotates; it's similar to the starter motor, but of course much smaller.

An extension of the armature shaft into the gearbox carries a worm, which engages with a gearwheel. This carries on its upper face a pin that drives a connecting rod, converting the rotary motion of the gear into a reciprocating motion — Figure 9.1(c).

Connected to the outer end of the crank is a crosshead block, which slides in a channel and is secured to the end of a spiral rack, which slides backwards and forwards in a Bowden-type steel tube. Spaced along the length of the tube are two wheelboxes, each one containing a gearwheel on a spindle mating with the spiral of the rack. The other ends of the two spindles protrude through the scuttle outside the car in the form of splined bosses, and on to these are fitted the wiper blades. The to-and-fro motion of the rack rotates the gearwheels to and fro also, causing the blades to move backwards and forwards over an arc on the windscreen.

Self-parking of the wipers is achieved by means of a 'parking switch' within the wiper gearbox, as follows. Inside the gearbox cover is fitted an insulating disc, which carries a brass disc with a small section cut out of it. A spring contact (finger) fitted to the crank pin on the gearwheel moves around the brass disc. This is connected to the motor in such a way that, when the wiper switch is turned to OFF, the circuit is maintained through the contact disc and finger until the wiper blades are at the end of their arc, usually along the lower edge of the windscreen. At this point the contact finger moves off the disc on to the insulated section, interrupts the circuit and stops the motor. The positioning of the insulated section is adjustable so that the motor stops with the blades in the correct position.

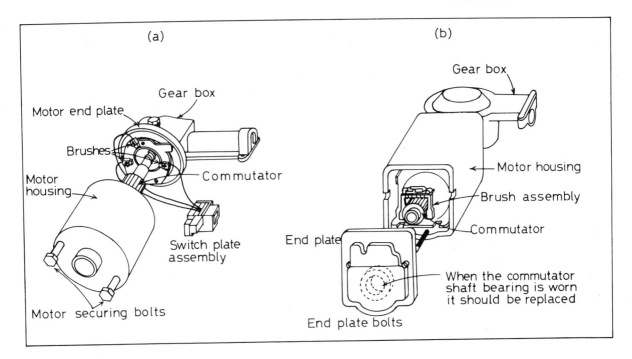

**Figure 9.1** Typical windscreen wiper drive: (a) permanent-magnet motor, (b) wound-field motor, (c) drive mechanism

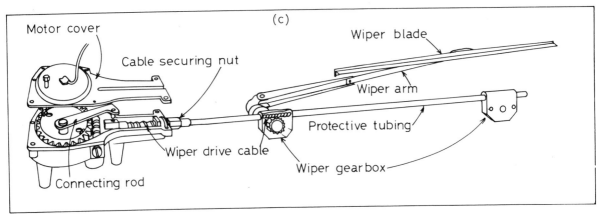

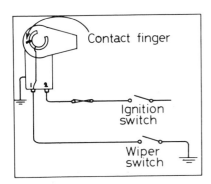

**Figure 9.2** Wiper motor parking-switch circuit

Unlike the lighting circuits on the car, the wiper motor is connected directly to the ignition-controlled fuse, so that one terminal becomes 'live' as soon as the ignition is switched on. The other motor terminal is connected to one switch terminal (and also to the parking switch of the motor) and through the switch to earth; see Figure 9.2. (Note that some earlier Lucas wiper motors and some Continental wipers are not fed 'live' continuously. Instead they are connected to earth, and the 'live' connection is made through the wiper switch in the same way as the lights. No self-parking switch is fitted to Lucas wipers of this type.)

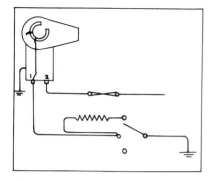

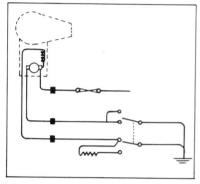

**Figure 9.3** (a) Two-speed wiper circuit, (b) an alternative method of obtaining two speeds

Closing the switch completes the circuit; the motor commences running and does so until the switch is opened again. Then the parking switch maintains the circuit until the required blade position is reached, when it breaks the circuit and the motor stops.

Two-speed or variable-speed operation can be obtained in various ways. In one, a resistor is incorporated in the switch circuit to the motor — Figure 9.3(a). It may be a fixed resistor, brought in or out of circuit by the switch, or a variable resistor incorporated in the switch or in the form of a separate switch. When the resistor is in circuit, it will have the effect of slowing the motor.

Another method is to bring one end of the field winding out to the switch (which is, in effect, a double switch) and to insert a resistance in the field circuit — Figure 9.3(b). This weakens the magnetic field in the motor and causes it to run faster.

The same effect is sometimes obtained by using a field winding with a centre tapping, so that either the full field winding or part of the winding is in circuit according to the switch position.

## Repairing a wound-field motor

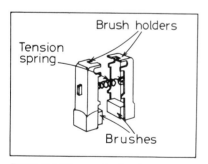

**Figure 9.4** Wiper motor brush gear

*If the motor fails to operate,* check for current to the motor with the ignition switched on. The green wire connected to the No. 2 terminal at the motor is the one to investigate. If this is 'live', connect the No. 1 terminal to earth. The motor should run; if not, the fault is in the motor (see below). If it does run, the fault is in the switch or in the wiring between motor or switch or between switch and earth. Check by connecting each switch contact to earth in turn.

If the motor does not run when the No. 1 terminal is earthed, switch off and remove the two long screws that hold the motor together. Remove the end cover. You will probably find that the brushes are worn out or even that the brush boxes have broken off. New brush assemblies are obtainable from Lucas agents and it's an easy, though fiddly, job to fit them (Figure 9.4). Don't forget to fit the fibre locking plate.

If the armature windings are burnt, or if the brushes have worn through the copper segments of the commutator, this means a trip to the Lucas agent for a replacement armature. Don't try skimming the commutator on a lathe: it's too thin to stand it.

To remove the armature, the yoke carrying the field coil must be pulled off with the armature, which can then be removed from the gearbox end of the yoke. When replacing it, pull the wire to the parking switch through as you go, so that it does not get trapped inside the motor.

When the armature and brushes are reassembled, take the gearbox cover off. mark the position of the parking switch, so that it can be replaced correctly, and check that there is a little end play on the armature shaft. About 0.25 mm (0.01 in) is sufficient. Some motors have an adjustable thrust screw and locknut.

At the same time check the teeth on the large gearwheel (they have been known to strip) and make sure that the gearbox grease is around the gears etc., and has not been pushed to the outside and dried up. Dab a spot of oil on the armature shaft when reassembling, but not too much at the commutator end.

*If the motor fails to switch off*, this is usually due to a fault in the parking switch or, more likely, due to the wire from the motor to the parking switch shorting to earth at the point where it emerges from the body of the motor to connect to the parking switch.

*Excessive movement (slack) in the wiper arms*, which causes the blades to bump the screen at the ends of the arc, can sometimes be cured by reversing the drive.

To do this, remove the gearbox cover of the motor and take off the spring clip securing the connecting rod to the pin in the gear. Lift out the connecting rod. (Never bend the end of the rod up to clear the drive rack.) Remove the wiper arms and blades. Pull out the drive rack (the wiper spindles will rotate as you do this) and when it's clear of the second spindle, turn it over: rotate the end through 180 degrees. Then rotate each wiper spindle through 180 degrees.

Push the rack back into position and refit the connecting rod, contact finger and spring clip. This operation brings the unworn side of the rack into mesh with the unused half of the wiper spindle gears, and should take up most of the slack in the movement (Figure 9.5). If the rack is dry as you withdraw it, smear it with HMP grease as you put it back.

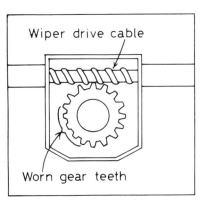

Wiper drive cable

Worn gear teeth

**Figure 9.5** Details of a wheel box

Replace the gearbox cover and blades and arms. If the blades are in the parked position before you start, they should automatically be correct after carrying out the operation.

*Very restricted movement of the wiper arms* may be due to the first section of the outer tube becoming detached either at the motor end or at the wheelbox end.

*If the motor runs when switched on but the blades do not move*, there are three possibilities. First, the teeth on the main gearwheel may have stripped and a new one will have to be obtained from a Lucas agent. Second, the crosshead block may have pulled away from the spiral rack. A new one will have to be obtained from a Lucas agent and fitted as described above in the paragraphs on taking up slack in the drive. Third, the gears on the wiper spindles may have worn. In this case, new wheelboxes, obtainable from Lucas, will have to be fitted.

The wheelbox is secured by the large nut just behind the wiper arm and by two screws (or nuts) that hold the cover plate at the back of the wheelbox. This plate also holds the outer tubing of the drive, and care must be taken when replacing the wheelbox to ensure that the raised lip on the end of the tube engages with the correct slot in the wheelbox on reassembly.

When renewing the main gearwheel (it is held in place by a circlip where the shaft protrudes through the gearbox housing), ensure that all washers are replaced in their correct positions and that the dished washer immediately underneath the gearwheel is the correct way round. This acts as a thrust washer to take up slack, and you will have to press the gearwheel home before you can get the circlip into place on the shaft.

Ensure that you buy the correct gearwheel. There is a number stamped on it, showing the angle of wipe of the blades: 110°, 130°, etc. If you fit the wrong one, you will find that either the blades hit the edges of the screen at the ends of their arc or that they do not clean a sufficient area of screen for good visibility.

Wiper blades should be changed regularly. The recommended interval is every 12 months. When the edge of the blade wears, the cleaning action is reduced and smearing results. Similarly, if the edge of the blade gets worn or cut by grit, the cleaning action will be streaky.

If the spring tension in the arms is reduced, the clearing action of the blades will be affected. To cure this, fit new springs (where possible) or replace the whole arm.

## Crank and linkage drive

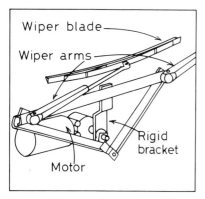

**Figure 9.6** Crank and linkage drive

Instead of rack-and-pinion drive, some cars have a crank-and-linkage drive. The motor assembly is the same, but instead of a crank pin and connecting rod to impart the reciprocating motion to the arms, the main gear spindle is extended outside the gearbox and a crank is fitted to the end of the shaft.

A bracket fixed to the gearbox carries a spindle housing and spindle each end. Each spindle also carries a crank lever (riveted on), and linkages connect these cranks to the main crank (Figure 9.6). As the main crank revolves, a reciprocating motion is imparted to the spindle cranks.

Wear in the linkage bearings can cause the cranks to drop over dead centre and jam. When this happens it can be rectified (to a certain extent) by fixing a light tension spring — or even a rubber band — in such a way that the linkage is lifted slightly at the end of the stroke to prevent it dropping into the jammed position.

One fault that repeatedly occurs is when one of the clips that secures the links to the cranks (particularly at the wiper spindle end) comes off and allows the link to slip off the crank.

**Permanent-magnet motors**

Mechanically, wipers fitted with these motors are the same as those with wound-field motors, and a permanent-magnet motor may be used with either spiral-rack or crank-and-linkage drive. Electrically, however, they are rather different.

In place of the wound field, which sets up a magnetic field when the motor is switched on, a powerful magnet is built into the body of the unit. This has two effects. First, speed control by varying the field strength is impossible, since the field strength is fixed. Second, the motor is reversible. Changing the direction of current flow by reversing the battery connections will not affect a wound-field motor; both armature and field magnetism are reversed, and so stay the same relative to each other. With a permanent-magnet motor, however, reversing the polarity will reverse the magnetic field of the armature but not of the field, and the motor will run in the opposite direction.

Thus, if you wish to change the battery polarity of your car for some reason, or if you want to fit a wiper motor of the PM type from another car of different polarity, wiper polarity has to be reversed. If this is not done, the motor will run backwards, affecting operation of the parking switch; also, since the thrust on the armature shaft, caused by the action of the worm drive, will be reversed, the armature will not rotate freely. The bearings are designed for rotation in one direction only.

Fortunately, polarity reversal is quite simple. All you have to do is to remove the two long bolts that hold the motor together, rotate the body of the motor through 180 degrees, and replace the screws. Don't lift the body at all, just turn it.

Speed control is achieved by using three brushes on the commutator instead of two. One is the earth brush, and the other two are energised separately by the switching system to give two speeds. The normal-speed brush and the earth brush put the full armature windings in circuit, while the fast-speed brush and earth brush only connect part of the armature, giving a higher speed.

Self-parking, again, is different from the method used with the wound-field motor. There are two stages (see below), operated by a cam on the underside of the main gearwheel. The cam engages with a small peg protruding into the gearbox from the switch.

Refer to Figure 9.7. With the wiper switch in the NORMAL position, wiper terminals 4 and 5 are connected, and current flows from 'live' terminal 4 through the switch to 5 and to the armature of the motor, then via terminal 1 to earth. In the FAST position, terminals 3 and 4 are connected by the switch and the circuit is through the offset brush.

In the OFF position, terminals 2 and 5 are connected by the switch and the circuit is from 'live' terminal 4 through the parking switch terminal A to switch terminal 2, through

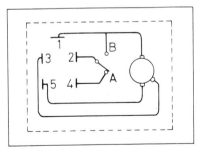

**Figure 9.7** Parking circuit for a PM wiper motor

the switch to terminal 5 and so through the armature. This means that the motor keeps running until the cam on the underside of the gear actuates the first stage of the parking switch, which breaks the connection between the switch blade and contact A. The motor, which is now switched off, still runs through a few more degrees under its own momentum until the second stage of the cam closes the switch blade on to contact B, which short-circuits the armature via the switch; this acts as a powerful brake.

The short-circuit through switch contacts 2 and 5 must be removed before the motor can be restarted, which is why a simple flick switch cannot be used for intermittent wiping: see later.

### Repairing a permanent-magnet motor

Maintenance is merely a matter of keeping the mechanism clean and lubricated, and repairs are limited to renewing the motor brushes when worn. To gain access to these, the body and magnet assembly must be removed. Mark the body first so that it is replaced the same way round, otherwise the motor will run in the reverse direction on reassembly.

It is also possible to renew the main drive gear if the gears should become stripped — normally due to lack of lubrication of the drive assembly. The parking switch can be renewed should the contacts fail. The switch simply clips into position on most motors. On earlier models, however, the switch is secured by two self-tapping screws inside the gearbox, and the main gearwheel has to be removed to gain access to them.

Running on when switched off is usually caused by failure of the parking switch.

If the fuse blows when the wiper is switched on, this is caused either by a failure of the parking switch or in the operating switch on the dashboard, particularly if it is of the rocker type. Disconnecting the green/brown and/or green/red wire will usually effect a temporary cure, enabling the wipers to be used but with no automatic parking. The blades will stop as soon as the switch is moved to OFF.

### Delayed or intermittent wiping

This can be achieved in several ways. Switching on and off manually is tedious; an alternative, if the motor is of the wound-field type, is to fit a spring-loaded toggle switch, which works under pressure only, similar to a headlamp flasher switch. When finger pressure is removed, the parking switch takes over to complete the wipe and switch off at the end of the stroke.

This method will not work with the permanent-magnet motor, as the wiper armature is short-circuited by the parking switch and the short circuit has to be removed before the motor can be switched on, complicating the wiring somewhat.

Electronic units have been introduced to do the job automatically. A transistorised circuit gives an impulse to the wiper motor at predetermined intervals, usually ranging from about three seconds to thirty seconds or more. The interval can be varied over the range by means of a rotary knob, which also switches the device on; then, once set, it will continue to give one wipe every few seconds until switched off.

Units are available to operate with permanent-magnet motors and also for Continental cars. It is essential to get the one that is suitable for your particular car. Full instructions are given with each unit for fitting and wiring. Keep these in a safe place after fitting, and you may be able to transfer the unit if you change your car.

**Electric screen washers**

These are small permanent-magnet motors that drive a small centrifugal pump fitted to one end of the armature shaft. They are usually wired in the same way as lights through the ignition-controlled fuse (Figure 9.8).

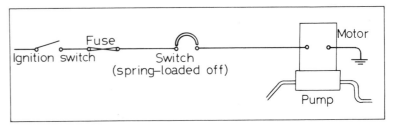

**Figure 9.8** Electric screen-washer circuit

Since the motor is a permanent-magnet type, it is essential that it is connected correctly (terminals are marked + and −). If connections are reversed, it will turn the wrong way and will not pump water.

Test by checking the earth connection. Connect one lead of a test lamp to the 'live' battery terminal. It should light. If it does, supply the motor directly from the battery by connecting a wire from battery 'live' to the other motor terminal. If the motor runs, the fault is in the switch section of the circuit. If it doesn't, the motor itself is faulty and it is not usually repairable.

Screen-wash motors are often connected to intermittent-wipe switches so that every time the wiper operates, there is a brief jet from the screen wash pump.

**HORNS**

There are three types: high-frequency, windtone and air horns.

The first two operate on the same principle (Figure 9.9). A metal diaphragm is fitted across the horn body, which contains an electromagnet. This is fed from the battery via a pair of contacts, which are normally closed.

E

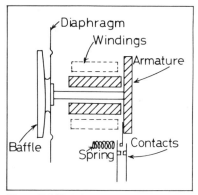

**Figure 9.9** High-frequency horn, shown in section

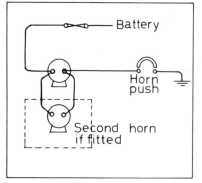

**Figure 9.10** Continuous live horn circuit

When the current is switched on by operating the horn push, the electromagnet is energised and attracts the armature which is attached to the diaphragm. As the armature and diaphragm move, a spindle pushes the contacts apart and breaks the supply of current to the windings. The diaphragm returns to its normal position with the armature, the contacts close and the process is repeated. The action is similar to that of an electric bell.

The whole thing happens very quickly. The frequency of the cycle is determined by adjusting the tension on the spring, and this in turn determines the note of the horn.

A baffle fitted to the front of the diaphragm of the high-frequency horn sets up vibrations in the air and thus generates the sound. In the windtone horn, a trumpet (either straight or coiled) contains a column of air, which is set in motion by the diaphragm to give the sound. This is a more mellow note than the rather harsh sound that the high-frequency type produces. Windtone horns are usually used in pairs, one with a high note and one with a low note, sounded simultaneously and matched to give a pleasant tone. Generally they are marked with an H and an L to distinguish them.

Most older cars have the horn (or horns) wired direct to the battery or fuse, so they are 'live' all the time. The horn push is wired in the earth or return circuit (Figure 9.10).

## Fault-finding

Earth one lead of the test lamp and connect the other to the fuse and the horn 'live' terminal in turn. The lamp should light. Now earth one end of a plain test lead, and touch the other to the second horn terminal: the horn should sound. If not the horn is faulty.

On some horns there is an adjusting screw. Turn this both ways a few notches at a time. If the horn then operates, turn the screw until the best note is obtained. If nothing happens, the horn must be replaced if it is a riveted type. Types that are held together with screws can be dismantled. Cleaning the contacts may give the horn a new lease of life. You may also find a broken wire that can be resoldered.

If the horn works on the above test, check at the connection to the horn push (snap connector or plug and socket) where wires from horn and indicator switch join the main wiring, close to the steering column. Remember that the horn wire is brown/black or purple/black. If the horn operates when this connection is earthed, the fault is in the horn push. If not, it is in the wiring between the horn and the junction under test.

Horn switches vary. Sometimes the switch is in the end of the stalk of the indicator switch. A fault in this type is

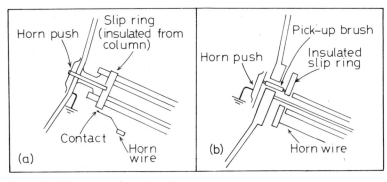

**Figure 9.11** Two types of steering-column horn push

difficult to rectify, unless it is a break in the wire where it emerges from the stalk. In this case, the broken end can sometimes be picked up and repaired.

A second type has a slip-ring connection to a horn push or horn ring on the steering column: Figure 9.11(a). A fault is probably mechanical in origin. It may be a bent contact finger failing to connect, or the contacts may have separated due to wear in the bearing bushes in the top of the steering column. A little judicious bending may rectify matters.

A third type has a slip ring mounted below the steering wheel and a spring-loaded pick-up brush in the wheel boss to carry the current to the horn push or ring: Figure 9.11(b). Dirt on the slip ring or a broken wire in the brush assembly is usually the culprit here.

The Triumph Herald and the TR models suffer a different kind of fault. There is a rubber universal joint between steering column and steering box, and the column itself is mounted in insulating blocks. A metallic braid connection across the universal joint is the only earth path for the horn circuit, and this corrodes and breaks in time. Access to the universal joint is not easy. To restore the horn circuit, the easiest way is to fit a strip of springy brass to the bulkhead just above the steering column in such a way that it bears on the column itself. Clean the column well at this point, to earth the steering column and complete the horn circuit (Figure 9.12).

On many later cars, the horn circuit is wired in the same way as the lights, i.e. with a 'live' feed to the horn push (which is insulated) and then to one horn terminal. The other horn terminal is earthed, or in many cases the earth connection is made directly through the body of the horn, with no second terminal and earth wire (Figure 9.13).

The connection to the horn push may be taken directly from the battery or via a fuse, or it may be taken from the ignition circuit so that the horn is 'live' only when the ignition is on. Use the same methods of testing as for lights (see page 66).

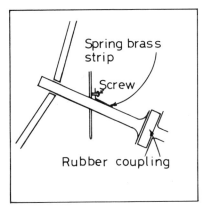

**Figure 9.12** Sprung brass contact method of earthing the steering column

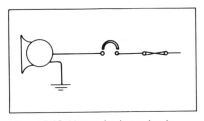

**Figure 9.13** Alternative horn circuit

**Air horns**

These operate on a different principle. Instead of the horn push working on the horn unit itself, it controls a small vane-type compressor, mounted on the end of an electric motor. Compressed air is led from the compressor to one or more horns, which operate in the same way as small trumpets. The length of each trumpet determines the note it produces, and a set can be arranged to give a pleasant chord. (In some cases, in conjunction with a rotary valve in the compressor, a set can give single notes in sequence to play a tune. The unit will be supplied with one tune in mind, but by re-arranging connections of the tubes between compressor and trumpets it is often possible to play something else. See the note on horns in Chapter 12, however.)

The compressor can be connected directly to the horn push — either the standard horn push (to operate air horns instead of those fitted as standard) or a separate horn push, fitted as an extra to the instrument panel. In this case fault-finding is as for the standard types of horn. It is, however, more normal to fit a relay in the circuit to relieve the load on the horn-push contacts. Relays are dealt with more fully in Chapter 10.

A second switch (usually referred to as the tone-control switch) is fitted with most multi-trumpet air horns. This alters the operation of the rotary valve so that, instead of playing a tune, the horns sound a single chord (Figure 9.14).

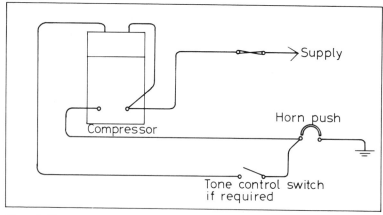

**Figure 9.14** Air horn wiring

**ELECTRIC PETROL PUMP**

Inside the body of an electric petrol pump are the valves and the petrol chamber. Sealing the latter is a diaphragm with a steel armature disc fitted to the centre and a long brass rod that passes through the core of a solenoid winding enclosed in the body of the pump. At the top of the pump is the contact assembly, the moving contact being fixed to the dia-

phragm spindle. You can see the general layout of parts in
Figure 9.15.

In the 'normal' position, the diaphragm spring pushes the
diaphragm towards the base and the contacts are closed. On
switching on the ignition, the solenoid windings are energised
and the armature is drawn towards the core, pulling the diaphragm with it.

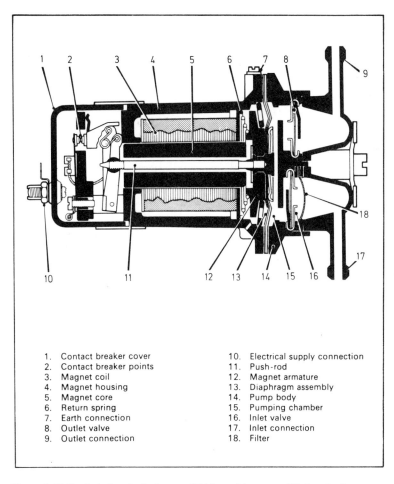

| | |
|---|---|
| 1. Contact breaker cover | 10. Electrical supply connection |
| 2. Contact breaker points | 11. Push-rod |
| 3. Magnet coil | 12. Magnet armature |
| 4. Magnet housing | 13. Diaphragm assembly |
| 5. Magnet core | 14. Pump body |
| 6. Return spring | 15. Pumping chamber |
| 7. Earth connection | 16. Inlet valve |
| 8. Outlet valve | 17. Inlet connection |
| 9. Outlet connection | 18. Filter |

**Figure 9.15** Typical electric fuel pump (SU-Butec) (courtesy B L Cars Ltd)

As the diaphragm moves away from the base, petrol is drawn
into the chamber through the filter and inlet valve. The spindle
attached to the diaphragm pulls the inner rocker of the contact mechanism until the trip or rocker springs 'throw over',
moving the outer rocker downwards to separate the contacts.

The solenoid is de-energised and the diaphragm spring asserts itself, pushing the diaphragm back and forcing petrol out through the outlet valve and into the carburettor.

When the diaphragm reaches the end of its stroke, the contact throw-over mechanism operates again, the contacts close and the process is repeated until the carburettor is full. At this point, the back-pressure of the float on the needle valve prevents the spring from forcing any more petrol into the carburettor. As the fuel level in the carburettor drops, the needle valve opens and the spring pushes the diaphragm further, to force more petrol into the carburettor, and so on.

*Note*: it is the pressure of the diaphragm spring that pushes the petrol into the carburettor; the electrical action of the pump merely loads it with petrol.

There are several types and sizes of pumps. Some are low-pressure, some high-pressure. Some are single, some twin pumps on a single base, etc. Both the operation and the procedure for repairs are the same.

**Dismantling and repair**

The most likely problems are either concerned with the diaphragm or with failure of the contact points.

Diaphragms occasionally become porous and leak. There is also the possibility that, if left standing for a very long period, the diaphragm may become stiff and prevent the pump from operating. In both cases the solution is to fit a new diaphragm.

Contact failure is due to wear. In many cases, cleaning and adjusting the contacts will get the pump operating again, but if the contact faces are really bad, a new contact set will have to be fitted.

First remove the cover to expose the contacts and note how they are assembled. Remove the small screw securing the blade contact and remove the blade. This is in direct contact with the plastic base, and has all the washers, tags etc. on top of it.

Take out the six screws securing the body to the base, first marking the edges at the joint, so they can be reassembled in the same relative position. This is important on some pumps: if not done, the valves may not seat properly.

Separate the body from the base. It may be stuck at the joint, but treat it carefully. Unscrew the diaphragm and re-move it, together with the spring. Note which way the spring goes, i.e. with the wider end into the body.

Take care of the eleven (yes, eleven) brass rollers if your pump has them. Some pumps have a plastic roller assembly instead. The rollers have curved edges; they are actually a slice through the centre of a ball, and act in the same way (over a limited travel) as a ball bearing to centralise the diaphragm and to ensure that it moves freely in operation.

Remove the pivot pin that secures the contact set to the rear legs of the contact base. Remove the base-securing screw that holds the earth tag. Slacken the other screw and remove the contact set.

Clean the parts you are going to use again and fit the rocker section of the contacts into the contact base, making sure they can move freely. Check that the flexible wire from the contact assembly to the earth screw is not pulled tight.

Do not overtighten the big base-securing screws or you will crack the base, and note that the spring washer on the earth screw goes under the tag on the flexible wire. Don't fit the blade yet.

Fit the diaphragm and spring. If your pump has the plastic roller assembly, fit this on to the diaphragm armature first. Enter the screwed end of the spindle into the centre roller of the contact assembly and screw it in about four turns.

Now comes the important part. Continue screwing the diaphragm in and, after each turn, hold the body of the pump with both hands with the thumbs on the disc in the centre of the diaphragm. Press inwards, and the rocker assembly should throw over. Screw in another complete turn and check again. Repeat until the rocker does *not* throw over.

Now unscrew the diaphragm one hole (one sixth of a turn) and check again. Repeat until the contact *does* throw over. Screw in one hole to check — it shouldn't throw over. Come back one hole — this time it should throw over. If this is correct, unscrew four holes. This is the final setting.

Replace the eleven rollers, ensuring that they are correctly seated in the groove. Place the body on the base in the correct position. Make sure that none of the rollers has slipped out of position to prevent the body seating correctly. Insert the screws, making them just finger-tight.

Slip the end of a small screwdriver under the centre roller of the contacts, and lift up as far as possible so that the contacts throw over. This pulls the diaphragm into its working position. Now tighten the screws: tighten every other screw at first, and then the other three. Release the diaphragm and go round all six screws at least twice, tightening as you go.

Check the throw-over by lifting and releasing the centre roller with the small screwdriver. If all is well, fit the contact. If not, repeat the adjusting process.

Check the valves by blowing through the pump. You should be able to blow through the inlet union but not through the outlet union.

In the normal position, the blade contact should be just lifted off the base of the moving contact, and in the throw-over position the contacts should be separated by about 0.4 mm (0.015 in).

Refit the cover, and check the pump by connecting across a battery. It should hammer away steadily until one of the unions is obstructed, when it will slow down. Refit to the car and all should be well.

*Remember*: adjust the diaphragm before fitting the blade. Unscrew the diaphragm the correct amount. Stretch the diaphragm before tightening the screws. Make sure the rollers are in place and not trapped. Make sure the flexible earth wire is not tight.

## HEATER BLOWER

This is a small electric motor carrying a fan or impeller and built into the heater unit. The switch is usually in the 'live' side of the circuit, but is occasionally wired in the earth side, with the motor connected directly to the ignition circuit (or fuse).

Very often a resistance is incorporated in the circuit to give two-speed operation. Some types have a variable resistance to give a variable speed (Figure 9.16).

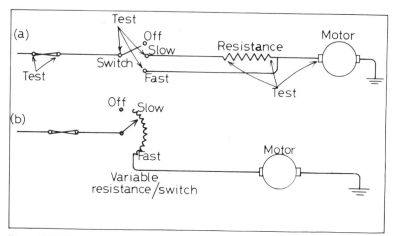

**Figure 9.16** Heater-blower circuits: (a) two-speed, (b) variable-speed

Test for circuit faults at the points indicated in Figure 9.16. The only part that can be replaced to repair a faulty motor is the set of brushes. Any other fault means a replacement motor, and no other spares are generally available.

A common cause of failure is broken glass from a shattered windscreen, or other small objects like coins etc., which fall down demister ducts and work their way into the impeller, jamming the motor. Neglecting this can cause the motor to overload and burn out.

Getting a blower motor out varies from car to car. Some are simple, and in others it means removing the whole heater unit. The heater is usually held together with self-tapping screws, but when dismantling make a careful note of how it fits together or you may have a few bits left over when you rebuild. Note the motor connections also, as many later motors are permanent-magnet types: if wrongly connected, they will run in reverse and won't blow hot or cold air where it is wanted.

## CIGAR LIGHTERS

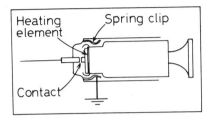

**Figure 9.17** Cigar-lighter circuit

The circuit for these is simple: a direct wire to the unit, usually through the auxiliary terminal of the ignition switch. This becomes 'live' when the ignition key is turned to the accessory position or ignition position, but is not connected to the ignition circuit itself. It is used for supplying accessories that may be required when the engine is not running — radio, cigar lighter, etc.

The cigar-lighter switch is incorporated in the unit (Figure 9.17). It's not really a switch, but a push contact made when the lighter element is pushed in. It's held in position by spring clips; as the element heats up, the spring clips expand and release the element so that it pops out.

If it doesn't work, check for current to the centre terminal and earth connection to the body of the unit. If these are sound, the element is faulty and must be replaced.

## OVERDRIVE

This is basically a simple circuit, but it does vary in detail between one car and another.

In its simplest form it consists of a solenoid that operates the overdrive unit through a simple plunger and lever linkage.

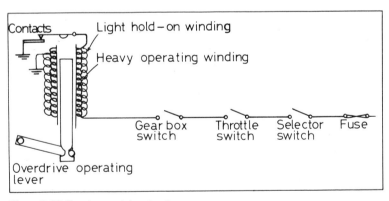

**Figure 9.18** Simple overdrive circuit

The solenoid has two windings: a heavy operating winding and a lighter hold-on winding. When the solenoid is operated, the heavy winding pulls the armature into the coil, the attached plunger moving up and pulling the overdrive operating lever with it (Figure 9.18).

At the end of the stroke, the heavy winding contacts are opened, leaving the hold-on winding (which takes far less current) to hold the overdrive engaged. When the overdrive is switched off, the armature and plunger return to normal and the contacts close ready for the next operation.

The gearbox switch is closed when the gear lever selects third or fourth gear; the throttle switch opens when the throttle is kicked down hard (often known as the kick-down switch) to cut the overdrive out for rapid acceleration (equivalent to dropping into a lower gear); and the selector switch on the instrument panel, steering column or gear lever switches the overdrive on or off as required.

Testing for a fault is carried out stage by stage, using the test lamp from one switch to the next until the overdrive solenoid is reached. If the solenoid does not operate, even though current is reaching it via the switches, the fault could be internal. The heavy winding contacts may not be closing properly; this is cured by checking and adjustment. The heavy winding may be broken; replacement is the answer here. The fault could be mechanical, i.e. the overdrive mechanism is stuck, in which case the fuse blows. If the solenoid keeps pulling in and out of engagement when energised, this is due to a fault in the hold-on winding.

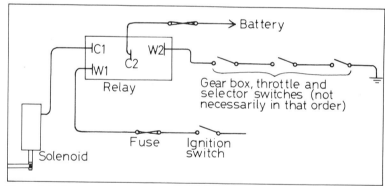

**Figure 9.19** Overdrive circuit incorporating a relay

A more usual circuit for the overdrive uses a relay to actually energise the solenoid, and the controlling switches are used to operate the relay (see the part of Chapter 10 dealing with relays). In this case, the seitches are in the earth circuit of the relay, which is fed 'live' from the ignition switch or fuse.

Referring to Figure 9.19, terminals C1 and C2 of the relay are the contacts that close when the winding between W1 and W2 is energised.

## RADIATOR FAN

This cooling device incorporates a small motor (sometimes a modified windscreen-wiper or blower motor) that drives a fan mounted usually in front of, but sometimes behind, the radiator. On bigger cars, two units mounted side by side are often used.

The idea is to enable the engine to reach its working temperature faster, by not having a stream of cold air blown through the radiator by a fan driven from the crankshaft pulley by a belt.

Not only does the engine warm up faster, usually with some saving of fuel (since a cold engine uses more petrol than a hot one) but the extra brake horsepower required to drive the fan, which can be quite considerable, is also saved; this again results in some fuel economy.

The fan is switched on and off by means of a thermal switch fitted in the cooling system, either in the radiator or the cylinder head, often with a manual override switch in case of switch failure.

The circuit is basically simple. A direct feed to the motor, from either the ignition switch or the fuse, is used. The other motor terminal is then connected to earth via the thermal switch. The manual switch is also connected between the second motor terminal and earth (Figure 9.20). This system has the drawback that, if the manual switch is left closed, the thermal-switch system is inoperative.

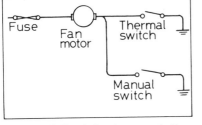

**Figure 9.20** Circuit for thermostatically controlled cooling fan

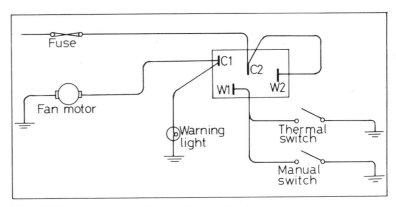

**Figure 9.21** Radiator cooling fan circuit with relay

A refinement in the form of a relay is often incorporated. Again, a manual switch is sometimes used as an override, but in this case a warning light is also wired in circuit and the switches and relay are in the 'live' side of the circuit (Figure 9.21).

Closing either the manual or the thermal switch energises the relay winding between terminals W1 and W2, thus closing the contacts and allowing current to flow from the ignition fuse via the relay contacts C1 and C2 to the fan motor and also to the warning light, which will be lit all the time the fan motor is running.

Remember that many fan motors are permanent-magnet types and must be connected correctly to prevent them from running in reverse.

To test the circuit, supply the fan motor with a direct feed from the battery, using a test lead to the 'live' terminal. If the motor runs, the fault is in the switch or relay circuit. See the relays section of Chapter 10 for the test procedure.

If the motor does not run, check the earth connection. If this is in order, the fault is in the motor itself and details of what can be done about this are the same as for the wiper motor.

# 10 Adding extras

The basic circuit for the majority of accessories is the same as for lighting circuits, i.e. simply a supply of current from a suitable source to one terminal of a switch, from the other terminal to the accessory, then usually through the body of the accessory to earth. But there are a few things to bear in mind.

Firstly, is the accessory to be controlled also by the ignition switch? This is all right for something like an electric windscreen washer, which will normally only be used when the car is in motion, but not for a radio, which you may want to use when parked.

Secondly, will the source of supply carry the extra load? The current for an accessory controlled by the ignition switch has to be passed through the switch contacts, and there is a limit to what they can stand without overheating or burning out. The same goes for fuses, which have a limit to the current they will carry without blowing.

Thirdly, wires of different carrying capacities are used in a car's circuitry, and again there is a limit to the current they can carry without getting hot.

**FUSES**

On many cars two fuses are fitted, usually rated at 35 amps; this is the maximum current they will carry before they blow, but for a short period only. Some components draw a considerable current for a very short period (e.g. an overdrive solenoid) but as soon as the initial operation is over, the current draw is greatly reduced to a figure well within the continuous carrying capacity of the fuse, usually about half the maximum figure. Many fuses are now marked with both figures. The small ceramic type of continental fuse with conical metal ends joined by a strip of metal is marked with its carrying rating, and the maximum rating is double this. A fuse marked as eight amps will carry current up to this figure continuously, but it will not blow on a temporary overload until 16 amps is reached.

Of the two 35 amp fuses normally fitted, one is connected directly to the battery to supply the horn and interior light. The other is connected, via the ignition switch, to feed direction indicators, brake lights, windscreen wiper and electric washer, instruments, and heater-blower motor. If any extras are added to these fuses, you should make sure the circuit will not be overloaded when they are switched on continuously, particularly the ignition-controlled fuse. Items such as horns, brake lights, and direction indicators can be ignored when working out fuse-carrying capacities, as they are only used intermittently and are not counted as part of the continuous load.

Many cars have an auxiliary position on the ignition switch that can be made 'live' without the ignition circuit being on — useful if you want to use the radio when parked. Some cars, such as Vauxhalls, have a fuse for this circuit, too.

A common fault is for too many items to be connected to the ignition-controlled fuse, particularly if a heated rear window is fitted, for this draws a fairly heavy current. The overload is usually insufficient to cause the fuse to blow, but the contacts between the fuse cap and the clips that hold it become overheated. This can cause the fuse to blow (melt), or in extreme cases can melt the fusebox, with a circuit failure as a result. It is often preferable to transfer the connection for the heated rear window from the ignition fuse (No. 2 in the fusebox) to the auxiliary fuse (No. 1). It will still be controlled by the ignition switch, so it cannot be left on inadvertently to run the battery down, but at the same time the load on the ignition fuse will be considerably reduced.

A limited number of accessories can be connected to the existing fusebox, but if you intend to fit several extras, or if your car has no fusebox, it is a good idea to fit another one. Several types of box are available from accessory shops and auto-electricians, and the small Lucas unit used on many cars is ideal for this purpose. It carries two fuses, which can be connected so that one is supplied directly from the battery and the other through the ignition switch, or both could be supplied through the ignition switch, or both could come from the battery, or you could even supply one fuse from the side-lamp circuit.

## WIRING HINTS

If you are going to fit extras, decide first what accessories you want and what you may wish to fit in the future. A certain amount of dismantling has to be done — trim panels, seats, and similar fitments — so as to run the wiring through in a safe and tidy manner. If you are wiring up for, say, a reversing light, it is a good idea to run extra wires while you are about it for other accessories such as rear fog-warning lights, rear-window wiper, or heated rear window. If you do this, the wires can be bound together to form a small wiring harness to run alongside the main wiring. The wire you wish to use can be connected up and the others tidied up until required.

Always use the correct type of cable for connecting up extras. There is a standard colour coding for all car wiring and adherence to these colours makes fault finding so much easier.

Wires come in different sizes and carrying capacity, the most common being:

- 65/.30 for main feed cables from battery to ammeter and for the alternator circuits.
- 44/.30 for feeds to control boxes, dynamo circuits and so on.
- 28/.30 for heavier load circuits such as headlights and horns.
- 14/.30 for nearly all other circuits, side and tail lights, stop lights, indicators.
- 9/.30 is sometimes used for very lightly loaded circuits such as instrument-panel lights.

In all these cable sizes, the first number denotes the number of strands of wire in the cable, and the second figure is the diameter of each strand in millimetres. For instance, 14/.30 cable has 14 strands of wire, each being 0.30 mm in diameter. (Before metric sizes were introduced, strand diameter was measured in thousandths of an inch. The equivalent of 0.30 mm is twelve thousandths or 0.012 in; thus the metric size 14/.30 is 14/.012 in the old system, and similarly for the other sizes listed above.)

Most auto-electricians carry stocks of coloured cable and should be able to supply those you want, so choose cables to suit the job, decide where they are going to run, and tape up those that will run together.

As far as possible, run new cables alongside existing ones, passing them through the same rubber grommets if there is room. If you have to drill a fresh hole, *always* fit a grommet, otherwise the bare metal will soon chafe through the insulation and you will have a short circuit. Fit the correct type of terminal to a cable end for connecting to fuseboxes, switches and so on, and remember that cable ends for those on heavier circuits should be soldered. This is particularly important on charging circuits, where a bad joint could cost you a new alternator.

Connect cables with bullet-and-sleeve snap connectors; crimped-type bullets are available, but a soldered one makes a better job.

*Never twist two ends of wire together to make a joint* except as a get-you-home effort. Always use proper connectors, except when repairing a wiring harness as described in Chapter 1.

**Soldering**

Soldering is easy with a little practice, the main essentials being cleanliness and correct heat. The slightest trace of oil or corrosion on a wire or terminal will prevent the solder running to make a good joint. The soldering iron must be big enough for the job otherwise the metal in the cable, especially

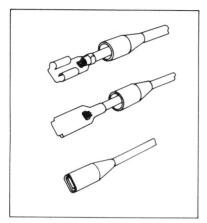

Figure 10.1 Stages in fitting spade-type terminals

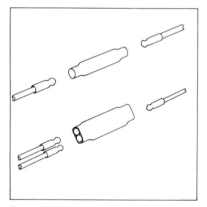

Figure 10.2 Using bullet terminal and snap connector to join wires and also to join in new wiring, using a double snap connector

heavier cables, will conduct the heat away faster than the iron can supply it and the solder will not flow into the joint.

Very small radio-type electrical irons are not much good for auto-electrical work, except for repairing printed circuits and similar jobs. A 150-watt electrical iron will do most jobs, but for really heavy cable (65/.30) a 250-watt iron is needed — or else a hefty (about 250 grams, or 8 oz) gas-heated iron to get plenty of heat to the joint.

When fitting a terminal to a wire (Figure 10.1), make sure that both are really clean. Insert the bared end of the wire into the inner clips of the terminal and squeeze the clips on to the wire with thin-nosed pliers. Now take the soldering iron and touch the end of the soldering wire (use resin-cored solder for all electrical work) to the tip so as to tin it, then press the tip of the iron to the joint together with the end of the solder wire. If the iron is at the correct heat — and an electrical iron should be — the solder will melt and run into the joint almost like water. If it is thick and sluggish the iron is not hot enough. Don't apply too much solder, just enough to colour the joint silver but not enough to form a blob. Practice makes perfect, so keep practising on old bits of wire!

When the terminal tag has cooled, squeeze the outer clips on to the cable insulation to secure it firmly in place. It is a good idea, though not essential, to fit a plastic sleeve over the terminal, in which case it must be slid over the cable before fitting the terminal.

If you are attaching soldered-type bullets (Figure 10.2), bare the end of the wire about 13 mm (½ in) and then slide the bullet into place so that the bared end protrudes. Now, hold the cable between the jaws of a vice so that the bullet is resting vertically on top of the jaws. Apply the soldering iron and solder to the tip of the bullet and the protruding wire until the solder runs into the joint. Allow to cool and remove from the vice. This method prevents the bullet sliding down the wire as the insulation softens from the heat of the iron. If you are doing the job on the car, hold the wire in the jaws of heavy pliers or a Mole wrench to conduct the heat away.

When soldering blade-type connectors, do it with the blade pointing upwards: this prevents the solder running into the grooves, which could stop you getting it on to the tag.

## USE OF RELAYS

Relays are needed in several accessory circuits; they are simply remote-controlled switches, working on the same principle as a solenoid. Whereas the solenoid may be used to operate something mechanically, such as a pre-engaged starter, as well as acting as a switch, the relay just opens and closes contacts in a similar manner to the cut-out and voltage regulator in the charging system.

Many accessories require a fairly heavy current, and a switch on the instrument panel would need to have heavy contacts to carry it. Also, if the accessory is some distance from the switch there will be a considerable voltage drop due to cable resistance, reducing the efficiency of the accessory, unless a heavier cable is used. Fitting a relay close to the accessory, with contacts that will carry the heavy current, will overcome the problem since the relay needs only a very small current to operate it.

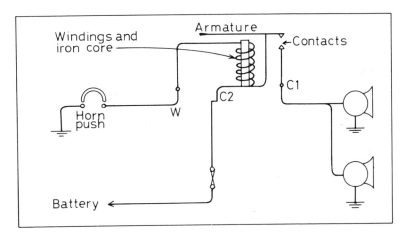

**Figure 10.3** Relay used in a horn circuit

For example, a pair of windtone horns can take up to **40** amps between them and this would soon cause the horn-push contacts to burn, but by introducing a relay the problem is solved (Figure 10.3). When the relay winding is closed by the horn push, a small current flows through the winding and sets

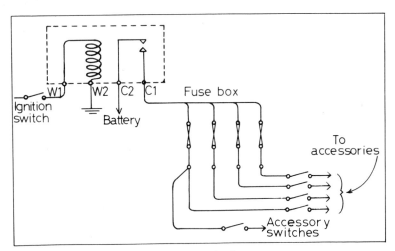

**Figure 10.4** Relay used to feed an auxiliary fusebox

up a magnetic field in the relay core, attracting the armature and closing the contacts. This allows the heavy current to flow through the contact and on to the horns.

This principle can be used in many other applications. For instance, where it is required to supply several accessories through the ignition switch, a relay can be used to feed an auxiliary fusebox. This means that the ignition switch does not have to carry the load, yet the accessories can still only be used with the ignition switched on. For this a four-terminal relay is used, with both ends of the coil brought out to the terminals (Figure 10.4), instead of one end of the coil being connected to the same 'live' feed as one of the contacts, as in the previous example. More than one accessory can be taken from each fuse if required.

## REVERSING LIGHTS

These are easy to fit, the wiring being a basic fuse-to-switch-to-lamp circuit. With many cars an automatic switch can be fitted into the gearbox, or else a manual switch mounted on the dashboard can be used. In the latter case, a warning light to show when the lamp is switched on is a legal requirement.

Some Ford reversing-light systems differ from conventional circuits by having the switch on the earth side (Figure 10.5). A single-terminal switch is used in the gearbox, the connection to earth being made when reverse is engaged. A double-pole bulb holder is used, instead of the normal single-pole one that earths through the lamp body. On some Ford systems the reversing lights are connected to the side/tail-light circuit instead of the ignition switch, since you are only likely to need them after dark. There is no reason why you should not do the same if you wish.

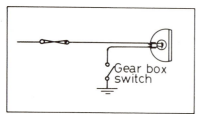

Figure 10.5 Ford reversing-light circuit with switch on the earth side

## FOGLAMPS AND SPOTLAMPS

Foglamps are best connected through a relay energised by the side/tail-light switch, since it is illegal to use foglamps unless the side lights are also on. This method prevents any mistakes (Figure 10.6).

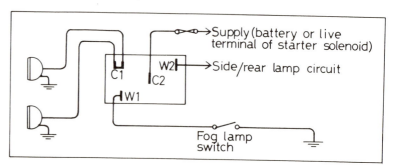

Figure 10.6 Foglamp circuit

Spotlamps are connected in the same way as foglamps, through the side-light circuit. A legal requirement for spotlamps is that they must be made to go out when the headlamps are dipped. One way of doing this is to connect the spotlamp switch terminal to the dipped-beam headlamp circuit instead of to earth (Figure 10.7). Alternatively the relay could be

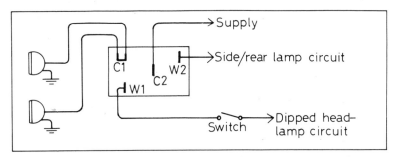

**Figure 10.7** Spotlamp circuit

connected to the main-beam circuit instead of to the side lights, and the switch put into the earth circuit, as for foglamps. This would also put the spotlamps out when the headlamps were dipped, but the spotlamps could not be used with side lights only.

**AUTOMATIC SIDE LIGHTS**

These are not often encountered, but devices are available to switch on the side and tail lights when conditions warrant it, i.e. at the onset of dusk or poor weather. A photo-electric cell controls a relay that does the actual switching. As the light fades, the cell circuit triggers the relay. A switch is incorporated to cut the device out when the car is parked.

**HAZARD WARNING LIGHTS**

Control equipment for hazard warning lights, to operate all four flashing indicators in case of a breakdown, is available as a kit. It consists of a multiple switch which, in one operation, connects the left and right indicator circuits together, connects the flashing indicators to a special flasher unit capable of supplying all four lamps, disconnects the normal flasher unit, and energises a warning light. This may sound complicated, but in fact the installation is quite simple if you follow the instructions. A typical circuit is shown in Figure 10.8.

The connection between the car flasher unit and the flasher switch is broken when the hazard warning is in operation, so there is no feed-back from the hazard warning to the ignition circuit.

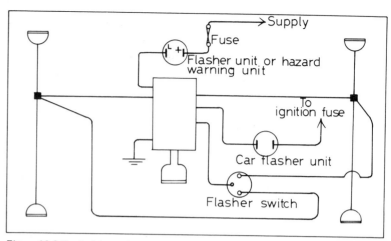

**Figure 10.8** Typical hazard warning light circuit

## BURGLAR ALARMS

No burglar alarm will stop a professional car thief, but they do deter sneak-thieves or someone who just wants to borrow the car to save a long walk.

Burglar alarms range from a simple concealed switch in the ignition circuit to something elaborate that flashes lights and sounds the horn.

The simple ignition cut-out switch is connected between the contact-breaker terminal on the coil and earth. This has the same result as if the contact-breaker points did not open (Figure 10.9).

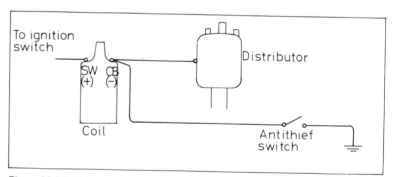

**Figure 10.9** Ignition cut-out switch used as a thiefproofing device

If the car has an electric petrol pump, a concealed switch can be inserted in the wire between ignition switch and pump. The car may start, but it won't go far on the small amount of petrol in the float chamber.

A more complicated system uses the door courtesy-light switches to control a relay that operates the horn if a door is opened (Figure 10.10). A key switch fitted in the side of the car is used to switch the alarm on after the doors have been locked. The key switch must be fitted in such a way that the terminals are inside the car and inaccessible from the outside: in the side of the boot is a convenient place.

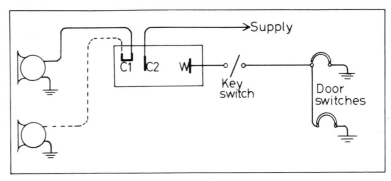

**Figure 10.10** Door-switch-operated burglar alarm

With this system the horn will sound if the doors are opened but they will stop as soon as the doors are closed again. A modification is to use a relay with a 'hold-on' contact. The hold-on contacts are connected across the door switch so that if the door is closed the circuit is maintained until the key switch is opened (Figure 10.11). The snag is that, although it may scare the thief away, you could find yourself with a flat battery when you get back.

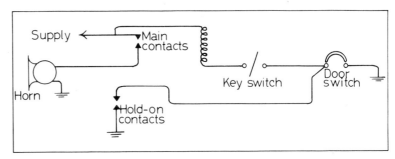

**Figure 10.11** Door-switch-operated circuit with hold-on contact

The previous systems you can make up yourself by buying the various bits, but you can also buy complete kits. Among these are the pendulum or vibrator operated systems (Selmar, Watchdog and others). These systems have contacts on a pendulum or vibrating spring; the contacts close if the car is rocked, and energise the relay and horn circuits. This type of alarm has the advantage that it deters someone from tampering with the outside of the car — stealing wheels, spotlamps and similar parts. The disadvantage, however, is that it can accidentally be set off by a passer-by bumping against the car, a heavy gust of wind, or even another vehicle going past.

**EXTRA HORNS**

Extra horns are quite easy to fit, either extra-loud ones (high-frequency or windtone) or air horns. The wiring is the same in each case, except that with air horns the wiring from the relay goes to a compressor unit instead of to the horns themselves: Figure 10.12(a). Full fitting and wiring instructions are included in the kits.

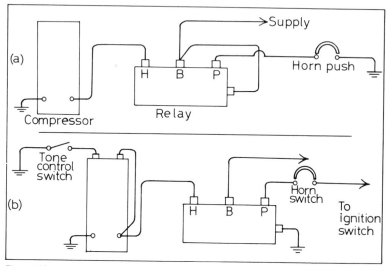

**Figure 10.12** Air-horn circuits

Some air-horn compressors, with three or more horns, have a relay circuit built into the compressor unit to operate the valves so that the horns can be made to play a tune of single notes (but see Chapter 12), or a blast with all the notes together. This type has two extra terminals on top of the unit, which are connected to a 'tone control' switch: Figure 10.12(b).

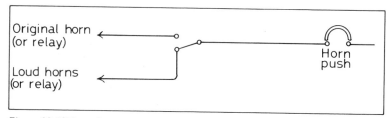

**Figure 10.13** Extra horns with changeover switch

You may also fit a changeover switch so that the original horns can be used for town driving and the louder ones for the country (Figure 10.13).

When you buy extra horns the relays may have different terminal markings to the Lucas type of relay, although they operate and are connected in the same way. Comparative markings are:

| Lucas | Bosch | Italian (Marelli) | Others |
|-------|-------|-------------------|--------|
| C1 | 87 | H | H |
| C2 | 30 | B | B |
| W1 | 85 | P | S |
| W2 | 86 | unmarked | — |

If the circuit requires a three-terminal relay and the relay you have is a four-terminal model, simply join C2 and W2 together.

## HEATED REAR WINDOWS

These are being fitted to more and more cars either as standard equipment or optional extras, but if your car is not already fitted with one there are several kits available for DIY installation.

Before fitting make sure the glass is thoroughly cleaned either with methylated spirit or a window cleaner such as Windolene. Stick the element on the window, pressing down firmly and working from the centre outwards.

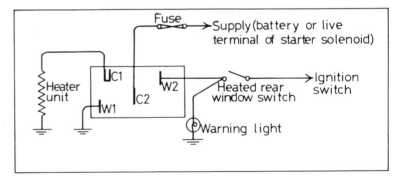

**Figure 10.14** Heated rear window with relay and warning light

Wiring is straightforward. Route the wire as for reversing lights, behind the trim wherever possible and not under the mats. Take the feed to the switch through the ignition switch or fuse. If possible, fit a relay to relieve the ignition switch of some of the load, as described earlier, and fit a warning light to show when the element is switched on (Figure 10.14).

The heater unit should not be left on for long periods, since it draws a fairly heavy current. On a car equipped with a dynamo, the total load with headlamps, wipers, heater blower etc. will be more than the maximum output of most dynamos and the battery will begin to drain.

## ELECTRICALLY-OPERATED WINDOWS

This facility is being fitted as standard on quite a number of cars these days, and kits are available to convert many other models — but not all, so check first.

The conversion is usually a bolt-on unit that engages the existing winder mechanism. The motor is reversible and is energised either by two relays, one for each direction of rotation, or by one double-acting relay. The relays are operated by a two-way panel switch, which is spring-biased to the 'off' position. Fitting instructions supplied with the kits are fully detailed and you should have no trouble installing the equipment.

## TRAILER WIRING

With plug and socket connections for trailers and caravans there is a standard system of connections to enable trailers and towing vehicles to be interchangeable. The terminals of the plugs and sockets are numbered; two systems of numbering are used, and sometimes both sets are used on the same socket (Figure 10.15).

Terminal 2 can be left vacant if not required. Terminals 5 and 7 are wired separately on the trailer, in case it is used with a vehicle that has the left and right rear lights on separate fuses. If both tail lights are on the same fuse, or if the circuit is unfused, only one connection from socket to rear lights is required and terminals 5 and 7 are joined together.

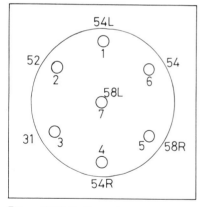

Figure 10.15 Trailer socket connections

| Terminal 1 | Yellow | Left-hand flasher |
| 2 | Blue | Live feed for caravan interior (if required) |
| 3 | White | Earth |
| 4 | Green | Right-hand flasher |
| 5 | Brown | Right-hand side/rear lights |
| 6 | Red | Stop lights |
| 7 | Black | Left-hand side/rear lights |

The connections from the socket to the lighting circuits on the car are made in the boot, at the rear-light junctions to the main wiring snap connectors. If the wiring goes direct to the lamp terminals the socket connections can be made either at the lamp terminals using piggyback connectors, or by cutting the wires and inserting snap connectors.

You can use either separate wires taped together into a harness, or the standard seven-core cable. The colour coding for the cable is shown above.

A heavy-duty flasher unit must be incorporated in the circuit instead of the existing one in order to cope with the extra load. Regulations demand also that an extra warning light is fitted, to show that the trailer flashers are working properly. Hella, Bosch and others supply suitable heavy-duty flasher units; the terminal markings are slightly different to the usual units:

49        Live feed from ignition fuse (B or + on old unit)
49a       Flasher unit to indicator switch (L on old unit)
C or C1   Original warning light (P on old unit)
C2        Extra warning light for trailer flashers

In some cases (Volkswagen for instance) a special unit is required, so check before buying.

When installed, the extra warning light should flash once when the indicators are operated without the trailer connected; they should flash continuously, in time with the original warning light, when the trailer is hitched up.

**ELECTRONIC IGNITION**

During recent years there has been a growing interest in electronic ignition as a means of getting better ignition, and there are now a number of devices that can be used to convert conventional ignition systems to electronic.

When an engine reaches fairly high revs, the spark at the plug of a conventional system tends to become erratic. There are two main reasons. First, the period of time during which the distributor points are closed becomes shorter as revs rise, until eventually the magnetic flux in the coil does not have time to build up to its full value; this weakens the high-tension spark at the plugs and can cause misfiring. Second, at high revs the spring loading on the moving contact may not be strong enough to keep the heel in proper contact with the distributor cams; the result is 'contact bounce', which again can cause misfiring. It was to overcome these problems that electronic ignition was introduced. In some cases it does away with mechanical contact points and replaces them with an optical or magnetic triggering system.

The earliest form of electronic ignition was known as the 'transistor assisted contact' system, in which the normal distributor contacts triggered a transistorised unit which energised the coil. This reduced the current flow across the contacts, diminished burning and stabilised the spark. It operated in a similar manner to a relay.

Although a big improvement over the conventional system, it still suffered from contact bounce and weakening of the spark at high revs, and it was soon superseded by the capacitive and inductive discharge system (Figure 10.16).

In the *inductive discharge* system, the transistorised unit is used to switch the coil, which stores the energy in a very

F

similar manner to the conventional system but much more efficiently. In the *capacitive discharge* system, the coil is used as a transformer, the energy being stored in a capacitor and triggered by the transistorised unit. Both types can be used in conjunction with either magnetic or optical switching in the distributor.

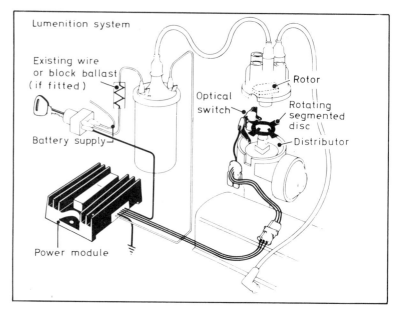

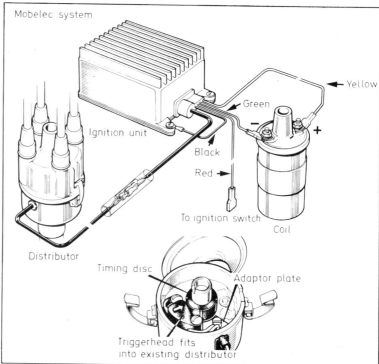

**Figure 10.16** Typical transistor ignition circuits

In the *optical* system, a small light source is separated from a light-sensitive unit by a disc mounted on the distributor spindle. The disc has slots in it corresponding to the cam lobes, and allows an interrupted beam of light to activate the light-sensitive unit. The tiny currents generated in it are amplified by the transistorised unit and used to trigger the system to generate the spark.

The *magnetic* system operates in a similar manner, except that in this case the lobes of the cam (Mobelec system) pass very close to a pick-up fixed to the base plate and induce a very small current in its primary winding; just as in the conventional coil, this induces current in a secondary winding. The current generated is amplified by the transistorised unit, which uses the coil in the usual way to deliver the high-tension pulse to the plugs.

These contactless systems give much better spark control, more accurate timing and (when matched to the distributor advance curve) improved performance and fuel economy, particularly on long, fast journeys. The improvement is not dramatic, and is less noticeable on short trips and in heavy traffic.

There are many makes available at widely differing prices depending on how sophisticated they are. Fitting instructions are given by the manufacturers, and after-sales service of the better-known makes is generally good.

# 11 Radio and tape players

Troubleshooting radios and tape players is far too much of a specialist job to be discussed in a book of this scope. It is, however, possible to buy and fit your own unit.

The range available is tremendous. It begins with a simple car radio, manually tuned with two wavebands (long and medium), often including a variable tone control and sometimes push-button wave change.

The next step up is the inclusion of four, five or six push-buttons for pre-set tuning. It's a useful facility to have but it does make the set more expensive — although prices for a six-button radio vary tremendously, usually dependent on other features like the quality of the circuit etc.

Tape-playing facilities can be purchased separately or as part of a combined radio/tape player, depending on personal preference. More popular these days is the cassette-type player, rather than the cartridge. Most equipment includes features like stereo sound, balance controls, variable tone control, manual cassette ejector and possibly fast wind and rewind controls.

At the top of the range, a unit will include long-wave, medium-wave and FM radio reception, the latter in stereo. This is linked to a stereo cassette player that enables you to record a stereo radio programme straight on to a cassette and then play it back later. This type of unit, however, is likely to be expensive and most people settle for something simpler and cheaper.

Before you rush out and buy your set, once you've decided how much you can spend and what sort of set you want, think about the car itself. If you've got a standard speaker slot provided, measure it (including the depth) to ensure you get a set that will fit.

Investigate the doors, if that's where you want to install loudspeakers. Some manufacturers provide mounting positions under the door trim, but on some doors it's almost impossible to achieve a satisfactory mounting without fouling the window-winding mechanism, door locks, etc.

If you decide on the rear parcel shelf as a mounting area for the speakers, remember that you will need a different shape and style. If you are fitting to the front foot wells, pod speakers could be the best bet.

Think also about the aerial position. Many manufacturers recommend the best spot for fitting, but generally it should be as far away from the ignition as possible. If the aerial is fully telescopic, there should be enough room under the wing or whatever for it to telescope into.

**INSTALLATION**

Once you've bought the set, speakers and aerial, there is a definite sequence in which to tackle the fitting. Start by disconnecting the battery. Fit the radio into the fascia but temporarily, so that access can still be gained to the back of the set. When it's all wired up, connect the speakers and fit the aerial, if possible, with an extension. Re-connect the battery, switch the set on and tune to a weak station. Now, grasping the aerial by the plastic insulated plug, touch it to various parts of the car while the engine is running. Find the spot where the interference is least, and that's where the aerial goes.

**Fitting the set**

Details will vary according to the set, the fitting kit and the car it's going into. Generally the set is supported at the front by nuts on the control spindles, usually involving some form of clamping plates or mounting plate. The support at the back of the radio may take the form of a foam pad resting on some firm part of the dash, or perhaps a drilled strip-metal bracket used as a bridge to an existing nut and bolt.

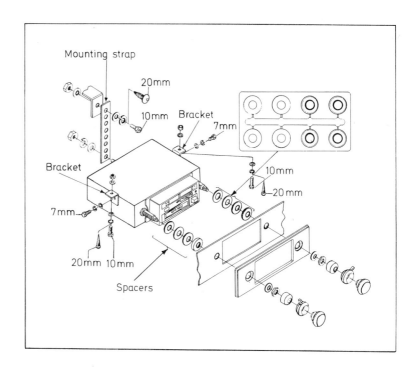

If the set has to go under the dash, a manufacturer's universal fitting kit will be used, incorporating either a saddle bracket or a pair of angle brackets. Fixing to the set is usually by means of drilled and tapped holes in its sides, with screws that are provided with the kit (Figure 11.1).

Fitting entails screwing the brackets to the sides of the set and then offering up in the position required. The brackets can be used as templates to mark through to the underside of the dash with a pencil or scriber. This is then drilled to suit either self-tapping screws or small BA nuts and bolts. To mask the ends of the brackets at the front, a moulded fibreboard fascia plate will be provided in the fitting kit.

In the absence of a fascia slot, and if there is no suitable under-dash position, the alternative is a centre console. These are available for most popular makes of car, and often incorporate a gear-lever shroud, an oddments tray and space for a clock, extra instruments, etc.

The power lead on many sets is permanently attached to a point inside the set, and on the 'flying' end is mounted half of the line-fuse carrier. The other half of the fuse carrier, with sufficient length of cable, is supplied and should be wired up to the accessory terminal on the ignition switch. This allows the radio to be used while the ignition is on or switched to the accessory position, but the set will go off when the ignition is off and the key withdrawn. The alternative is to wire up to a permanently 'live' point, either at the regulator or the fusebox. You must then remember to switch the radio off when leaving the car.

Use the proper terminals or Lucar connectors and solder or crimp them as required. See the relevant section in Chapter 10.

Earthing the set separately is generally a good idea, even if it is mounted on a metal fascia. With a plastic or wood dash panel, earthing is a necessity. Connect a short lead from one of the mounting screws to a known clean earth point. There is usually one already installed under the dash and used for earthing instruments.

Don't reconnect the battery or finish off the set mounting at this stage.

**Fitting loudspeakers**

If you have discovered manufacturer's mounting points, you will presumably be using these. They may be in the doors, at the ends of the fascia panel or in the parcel shelf. In most cases they are masked by blanking plates or by the trim. Pod-type speakers can be used at the ends of the front parcel shelf, or specially shaped surface ones can be used on the rear parcel shelf.

Door-type flush-fitting speakers can sometimes be fitted into the side trims of the front foot wells, or into the side trims at the back of a two-door car.

From the acoustic point of view none of the possible positions is very satisfactory. Foot-well, door, dash and under-seat positions all tend to be too low. Side panels alongside the rear seat are better, but rear parcel shelf mounting tends to throw the sound straight up at the back and over-accentuates the bass sounds because of the sounding-chamber effect of the boot.

Generally, side panels or the doors are the best compromise. If the manufacturer has designated a position, particularly if the metal has been cut away, use this. If not you will have to find your own best position — as high up the door as possible without fouling winder and latch mechanisms. There is also the possibility of water getting into the doors and ruining the speakers, so check window seals and drain holes in the bottom of the doors before fitting.

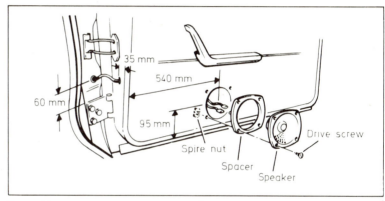

**Figure 11.2** How door speakers are fitted (courtesy Motorola)

Door speakers (Figure 11.2) are usually supplied with a fitting template. This is used to mark out the trim. It is obviously necessary to take the trim off first, however, in order to investigate the structure of the door behind it; this may mean removing handles, winder arms, armrests, ashtrays, etc. Mark the hole to be cut with chalk and then do the actual cutting using a Stanley knife.

If the only suitable position in the door is backed by metal, a hole will have to be cut. The professional tool for this is a power nibbling tool, but on a DIY basis the job is probably best done using a jig-saw attachment in the electric drill. If no such attachment is available, the job will have to be done by marking out the hole and drilling a series of interlocking small holes inside the line. The circle of metal is then knocked out and the hole finished off with files. This is a very tedious way of doing the job, however.

The actual speaker-mounting technique depends on whether the hole positions for the screws are backed with metal or not. If there is metal behind, drill a hole through both trim and metal and use a self-tapping screw for fixing. If there is no metal behind, use a self tapper with a spire nut to fix it to the trim only. The front speaker grille may be fixed by the mounting screws or some other method, depending on the make and style of speaker fitted.

The wiring is carried from the door to the door pillar, by drilling two 10 mm ($^3/_8$ in) diameter holes, one in the edge of the door and the other directly opposite it in the door pillar. Both holes are fitted with rubber grommets and the twin speaker fed through them. The part of the lead that is exposed should be protected by slipping a short length of plastic tubing over it: windscreen-washer tube is quite suitable. The rest of the wire is routed behind the front foot-well trim, up behind the dash panel and thence to the set.

Ensure that the two speaker leads are connected to the correct sockets on the set, or the balance control will work in reverse.

**Fitting the aerial**

Make sure that you buy a good-quality aerial. Usually you only get what you pay for, and it's best to spend extra money to get a good make. If it's a collapsible type, there should be some built-in device between the segments to ensure that contact between them is maintained. The base part should be metal, lined with plastic and with some type of drainage arrangement at the bottom. The other important point is that the screening of the co-axial lead must be adequate. It's copper and expensive and a cheap aerial might be a bit short in this respect.

The capacitance of the aerial must match the set. British and European sets should have an aerial of between 65 and 75 picofarads (pF). The figure for Japanese and American sets is between 95 and 110 pF. If you get the wrong one, there could be a 25 per cent signal loss.

The position in which the aerial is fitted is important too. A set supplied with a good fitting kit will often include precise instructions, including a template, for drilling the aerial mounting hole. Without this information, use the technique described earlier in the chapter to locate the site that is most free from interference.

The main operation is drilling the hole. Follow the instructions in the aerial fitting instructions; generally a 22 mm ($^7/_8$ in) diameter hole is needed. A good way to start is to cover the whole area with masking tape. This will make marking-out easier, and will help to avoid paintwork damage from a skidding drill bit or centrepunch.

There are many ways of cutting the hole, but the DIY man is presented with three main alternatives. One is to use a holesaw fitted in the electric drill. This entails drilling a small pilot hole to locate the holesaw, which is a ring-shaped saw that actually saws out the metal. Another way is to use a tank cutter. Again this is located on a pilot hole, and the tool is tightened with an Allen key until the metal circle drops out. The third alternative is the most laborious and the least accurate. This involves marking out the hole and then drilling a series of small holes inside the perimeter line. The hole is finally cleaned out to size, using rat-tail and half-round files.

The aerial will incorporate some sort of earthing device in its mounting assembly, probably a sharp-toothed clamp or perhaps a serrated ring. Ensure that the device is effective by cleaning away dirt, paint and rust from under the wing. When the aerial is finally in position, cover up the exposed metal with anti-corrosion primer or underbody sealant. Make sure, however, that you don't interfere with the good earth you have just made.

If you possibly can, take the aerial lead straight into the passenger compartment to the radio set *without* running it through the engine bay. This will cut down the chance of interference. Where the coaxial cable passes through holes drilled in the bulkhead, fit a rubber grommet to protect it against chafing.

Do not attempt to alter the length of the aerial lead. If it needs lengthening, buy a 'capacity-compensated' extension, of the same make as the aerial. If this is not done, there could be a severe signal-strength drop.

One more point, which you will have already thought about to some extent before buying: there must be room to accommodate the base of the aerial under the mounting point. Under a wing, for instance, check clearance above the road wheel, with the suspension in both the unloaded and the loaded position and with the wheels on lock.

Check also, before drilling, that the area is not double-skinned. This can make the job very awkward indeed, and is a complication to be avoided.

Plug the aerial into the set, when fitting is complete, and reconnect the battery. Switch the set on, tune it to a weak station around 200 metres on the medium wave, and turn the aerial trimmer. (This is a small screw fitted usually to the front of the set but sometimes elsewhere.) Turn it both ways until the loudest reception is found, thus matching the radio to the signal characteristics of the aerial.

The installation of the set, speakers and aerial can now be finished off. The job is complete, except for suppressing interference.

## INTERFERENCE SUPPRESSION

This part of the work could be simple, or it could be protracted and difficult and might eventually have to be sorted out by an expert.

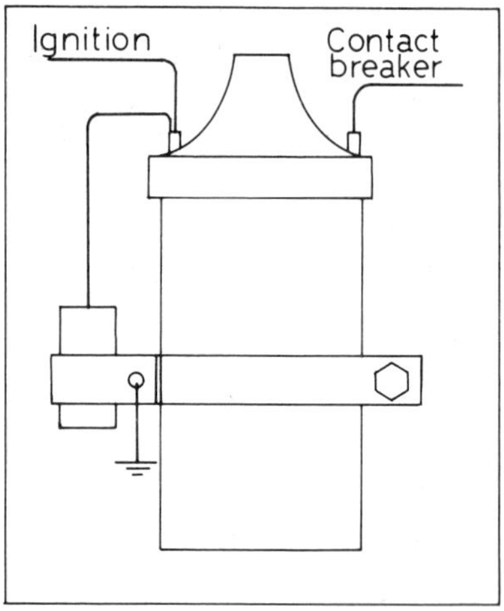

Tackle the ignition first. If your high-tension leads are the carbon-impregnated type, suppression should not be necessary unless they are faulty. If they are, interference will appear as a loud ticking sound, varying with engine speed. Fitting a new set of leads should cure this problem.

With copper-cored leads (generally considered more reliable from the ignition standpoint) resistor plug caps must be used, along with a line resistor in the lead between distributor and coil.

Fit a 1 $\mu$F capacitor between the SW terminal of the coil and earth. This is simple: the mounting bracket of the capacitor is bolted under the earth point and the 'flying' lead connection goes to the coil; see Figure 11.3. Clean the mounting bracket and the earth point so that good electrical contact is made.

If interference from the ignition persists, try more suppressors in the plug leads, either the in-line type or the sort that plug into the h.t.-lead towers on the distributor cap. You could also try resistive plug caps. Total resistance, however, in any single plug circuit should not exceed 25 kilohms. This is the total of the value of resistors in the coil lead, distributor cap, plug-in suppressor, in-line suppressor and plug cap.

Almost certainly you will need to suppress interference from the charging circuit. It is usually a whine, varying in pitch with engine speed and load on the electrical circuit. Fit

**Figure 11.3** Ignition suppression

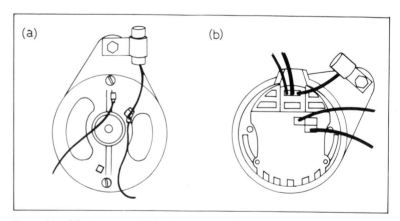

**Figure 11.4** (a) Dynamo and (b) alternator capacitors

a 3 $\mu$F capacitor between the main output terminal (thick wire) and earth. This applies to both alternator and dynamo (Figure 11.4). A 1 $\mu$F capacitor may be enough on the dynamo.

On the voltage regulator in a dynamo circuit, fit a 1 $\mu$F capacitor between the D terminal and earth (*never* to the F terminal).

The other electric motors on the car can prove to be a source of interference. Identify this by switching things on and off until the source becomes obvious. There are two things to be done. First, the motor casing can be earthed by means of a braided-metal earth strap. Second, a 1 $\mu$F capacitor can be fitted between the two motor terminals.

If the petrol pump produces interference, you'll need a 1 $\mu$F capacitor between the 'live' terminal and earth; if the voltage regulator in the instrument panel is the souce of the trouble, fit a 1 $\mu$F capacitor between the B terminal and earth (*never* the I terminal).

Earth-bonding straps can also be fitted to any part of the car that is electrically isolated from the main chassis by rubber mountings, cushioning rubbers, etc. Included in this are items like the bonnet and boot lid, bumpers, silencer, etc. Earth straps prevent them acting like an aerial, i.e. picking up and radiating interference.

Cars with glass-fibre reinforced plastic bodies have extra problems. With a conventional car, the metal-box structure of the engine compartment provides screening against interference. This effect can be imitated on a glass-fibre car by lining the interior of the engine compartment with metal foil, each piece bonded to the other with braided metal straps, and all bonded to the metal chassis at several places.

A cover to completely enclose the ignition system, made from sheet metal and bolted to the engine, will also help. Ventilation must be provided for heat from the engine by a number of 8 mm ($^5/_{16}$ in) holes; otherwise there is a risk of fire.

While the standard and basic suppression techniques will work well in 95 per cent of cars, there are always the few really difficult and obscure causes of interference. In these cases, it is usually worth consulting a radio-fitting specialist.

# 12 Electrics and the law

It is mainly the lighting system that is affected: regulations state just where and how many lamps may be fitted to a vehicle.

The normal side, tail, head and indicator lamps are fitted by the manufacturer in accordance with these regulations. It is when fitting extra lamps, or making changes to existing ones, that you must know just what the law allows.

The regulations are being modified and added to all the time, so it is always advisable to check before fitting anything out of the ordinary. Your local police station can usually supply the relevant information.

## GENERAL

● Headlamps, side lamps, tail lamps and stop lamps are obligatory and must be kept clean and in working order at all times.
● No head, spot or fog lamp may be mounted in such a way that it can cause dazzle at a height of 3 ft 6 in at a distance of 25 yards or more.
● Fog and spot lamps may be used in conjunction with headlamps or with side lamps only. If used in conjunction with headlamps, spot lamps must be switched off when headlamps are dipped.

## HEADLAMPS

● When two headlamps are fitted, they must be the same shape, size and colour (either white or yellow), and the centre of the lenses must be between 2 ft and 3 ft 6 in from the ground.
● They must both be capable of giving a dipped beam (unless they are switched off when dipped) and the dipped beam must be produced by two different lamps that are also within the prescribed limits. (See also under 'General' above.)
● On cars first used before 1 October 1969, the distance between the inner edges of the lenses must not be less than 359 mm.
● On cars first used after 1 October 1969, the distance between the inner edges of the lenses must not be less than 600 mm.
● On cars first used after 1 January 1972, the distance between the outer edge of the lens to the outer edge of the car must not be more than 400 mm.

• When four headlamps are fitted, the outer lamps must be capable of being dipped or must be permanently dipped. The others must give a main beam. All main beams must go out together when lamps are dipped.
• One single headlamp is illegal.
• When dipping, beams must deflect down or to the left.
• Headlamps must be switched on when driving at night on an unlit or badly lit road, or when weather or other conditions warrant it.
• It is illegal to leave headlamps switched on when the car is stationary (except at traffic stops).

**DRIVING (SPOT) LAMPS**

• These must be fitted with lamp centres between 2 ft and 3 ft 6 in from the ground. (See also under 'General' above.)
• On vehicles first used before 1 January 1971, the minimum distance between lamps and inner edges of lenses is 350 mm.
• On vehicles first used after 1 January 1971, the maximum distance from outer edge of the lamp to outer edge of vehicle is 400 mm.
• Lamps must be the same height, shape, size and colour (white or yellow).

**FOG LAMPS**

• The same fitting regulations apply, except that fog lamps may be mounted with lamp centres less than 2 ft from the ground, but in this case they must not be used except in thick fog or falling snow. (See also under 'General' above.)

**SIDE LAMPS**

• There must be two, showing to the front; they must be white, at equal height and the same size and shape. They may be incorporated in the headlamps (outer lamps on four-lamp sets). The lamps may not be mounted above a maximum height of 5 ft.
• The bulb may not exceed 7 watts.

**REAR LAMPS**

• Two red lamps are required, the same size and shape and at equal heights (between 1 ft 3 in and 3 ft 6 in from the ground) and not more than 1 ft 4 in from the vehicle's edge.
• Bulbs should be 5 watts.
• Two red reflectors are also required, and the same location regulations apply. These are usually incorporated in the rear light lenses.

**STOP LAMPS**

• Two are required, red in colour, and again they must be symmetrically mounted. Bulbs should be between 18 and 24 watts: 21 watts is more or less standard.

• The number plate must be illuminated in darkness so that the letters and figures are easily legible. (Many production cars have number-plate lights that do not conform to this regulation.)

## FLASHING INDICATORS

• These are compulsory on vehicles first used after 1 January 1971. For vehicles first used before 1 September 1965, the front indicators can be white or amber and the rear indicators red or amber. On vehicles first used after 1 September 1965, the front and rear flashers must be amber.
• The indicators must be symmetrical and must flash between 60 and 120 times per minute. A visual or audible warning must be given to the driver when they are switched on; if a trailer fitted with indicators is being towed, a second warning light must be fitted to show that the trailer flashers are operating.
• Height limits are between 1 ft 3 in and 7 ft 6 in from the ground.
• Semaphore indicators are still legal on older cars at present.

## REVERSING LIGHTS

• These are not compulsory. A maximum of two is allowed, and they may be used only when the car is reversing.
• The bulbs must not exceed 24 watts each, and the glass must be white and fluted — not clear glass. Only a diffused beam is allowed, so remove those spot lights used as reversing lights: they're illegal.
• Reversing lights may be operated automatically through the gearbox or manually; in the latter case, a warning light (which may be incorporated in the switch) is necessary.
• The lamps must not be left on when not reversing.

## SWIVELLING SPOT LAMPS

• These may be fitted for reading signposts, etc., but they may not be switched on when the car is moving.

## REAR FOG LIGHTS

• After 1 April 1980 manufacturers must fit two rear fog lights. On cars first registered before 1 April 1980 rear fog lights are not compulsory at present, but if they are fitted as an option they must comply with the regulations, which are:
• A maximum of two lights may be fitted.
• A single light must be fitted on, or to the right of, the centre line.
• If two lamps are fitted, they must be symmetrical, not less than 100 mm apart (between the inner edges of the lenses) and not less than 250 mm or more than 1 metre from the ground.
• They must emit a steady red light.

● They must be wired in such a way that they can only be switched on when side and tail lights are illuminated.
● They must have their own switch and warning light and may only be used in conditions of fog, severe spray and driving snow.
● They must not be connected to the stop lights.

## PARKING LIGHTS

● Cars may be parked on roads with street lamps with speed limits of 30 miles/hour or less without lights.
● On unlit roads or roads with speed limits of over 30 miles/hour, two side and two rear lamps are compulsory during the hours of darkness.

## HAZARD WARNING LAMPS

● The use of all four flashing indicators operating together is permitted if the car breaks down on a motorway or unlit road to warn of an obstruction.
● The use of hazard warning lights when the car is simply parked (for shopping etc.) is illegal.

## HEADLAMP FLASHERS

● According to the regulations, the use of headlamp flashers is to give a warning of approach in a similar manner in which the horn would be used. It should not be used as an invitation to another driver to proceed.

## HORNS

● The use of horns between 11 p.m. and dawn is illegal.
● Musical horns (i.e. those which play a tune) are illegal in the UK, although they may be used in some countries abroad. It is not illegal, however, to have them fitted to a car in the UK. They may be used in the UK if they are adapted to sound a single chord, i.e. all the notes are sounded simultaneously.
● Horns may not be sounded when the vehicle is stationary, and only when moving as a warning of approach. They should not be used as a gesture of annoyance or impatience or to attract the attention of friends on the pavement.

# Trouble tracer guide

| Fault | Possible cause | Test | Remedy |
|-------|----------------|------|--------|
| 1. All electrical circuits dead. | Battery fault (age or damage). | | Use jump leads, or borrow battery; replace battery. |
| | Flat battery, due to: faulty charging circuit | Check charging circuit (see items 8—15). | Use jump leads to start car; rectify charging fault. |
| | consumer units left switched on. | Check operation of boot light and under-bonnet light switches if fitted. On some cars (Rover) boot light does not always go out, due to distortion of switch mounting bracket or faulty switch. | Use jump leads to start car; rectify fault (if any) on consumer circuit. |
| | Corroded battery terminals. | Visual inspection. | Clean terminals. |
| | Loose or disconnected main feed cable. | Visual inspection. | Tighten or reconnect. |
| 2. Starter spins but does not engage. | Dirty starter drive, or damaged clutch in pre-engaged type. | Visual inspection. | Clean drive, or replace clutch unit. |
| 3. Starter engages but does not turn. | Starter jammed, due to worn pinion or flywheel ring gear. | | Try to turn squared end of starter shaft (clockwise to disengage), or rock car with 3rd gear engaged. Replace worn component. |
| | Partly discharged battery. | | As for flat battery (see above). |
| 4. Starter turns slowly. | Partly discharged battery. | | As for flat battery (see above). |
| | Engine earth strap corroded, broken or disconnected. | Connect jump leads between engine and battery earth terminals. Visual inspection. | Clean or replace earth strap. |
| | Faulty starter motor. | Remove and examine. | Repair or replace. |
| 5. Solenoid 'clicks' but engine does not turn. | Faulty solenoid contacts. | Bridge solenoid terminals. | If engine turns, replace solenoid. |
| | Solenoid-to-engine cable terminals loose. | Visual inspection. | Tighten or repair. |
| | Faulty starter motor | Remove and examine. | Repair or replace. |
| 6. Solenoid does not operate when ignition key is turned. | Faulty contacts in ignition switch. | Check with test lamp at terminals. | Replace. |
| | Wire disconnected or broken between ignition switch and solenoid. | Check with test lamp. | Reconnect or repair. |

| Fault | Possible cause | Test | Remedy |
|-------|----------------|------|--------|
| | Corroded or loose solenoid earth. | Check earth connection with test lead. | Repair as necessary. |
| | Faulty solenoid | Apply live feed from battery to operating terminal (white/red wire). | Replace. |
| 7. Starter turns engine, but engine does not fire. | **Petrol supply**<br>No fuel in tank.<br>Faulty petrol pump.<br>Blocked pipe.<br>Blocked carburettor jet. | | |
| | **Low-tension circuit**<br>No feed to ignition coil (faulty ignition switch; disconnected or broken wire). | Test at coil SW (+) terminal with test lamp. | Replace switch or repair wire. |
| | Faulty l.t. winding in coil. | Disconnect distributor lead. Test for current at CB (−) terminal. | Replace coil if test is negative. |
| | Disconnected or broken wire between coil and distributor. | Visual inspection. | Reconnect or repair. |
| | Distributor contacts not opening/closing correctly (wear or loose screws). | Visual inspection. | Adjust and tighten. Replace if necessary. |
| | Distributor terminal earthed, due to faulty condenser or wrong assembly. | Check assembly. | Correct if necessary. |
| | Distributor contacts burnt, due to faulty condenser. | Visual inspection. | Replace condenser and contact set. |
| | Distributor not earthing, due to corrosion or loose bracket. | Visual inspection. Check with test lamp. | Clean and tighten. |
| | Distributor contacts oily, due to excessive lubrication of distributor cam. | | Clean contacts. |
| | **High-tension circuit**<br>Faulty coil | Remove coil-to-distributor h.t. cable at distributor, and hold about 6 mm (¼ in) from engine. Turn engine or open and close distributor contacts by hand. If no spark between lead and engine, coil is faulty. | Replace coil. |
| | Faulty rotor insulation | Repeat previous test, but with lead from coil held to electrode on rotor. If there is a spark, rotor insulation is faulty. | Replace rotor. |
| | Faulty distributor cover (tracking to earth or between segments). | Visual inspection. | Replace cover. |
| | Fouled or wrongly gapped plugs | Visual inspection. | Clean, adjust gaps. Replace plugs if necessary. |

| Fault | Possible cause | Test | Remedy |
|---|---|---|---|
| **Dynamo systems** | | | |
| 8. Ignition warning light stays alight when engine is running. | Fan belt broken. | Visual inspection. | Replace, adjust tension. |
| | Faulty dynamo. | With engine running fairly fast, close cut-out contacts by hand. Bright blue flashes denote worn brushes and/or commutator. | Replace brushes. Skim and under-cut commutator as necessary. |
| | | If cut-out opens when released: (a) Faulty field coil circuit; test for continuity with lamp, including wire from control box (F) to dynamo. | Repair. |
| | | (b) Faulty connection from control box D to dynamo; brushes not contacting commutator. | Replace brushes. |
| | | (c) Faulty armature. | Replace. |
| | Faulty control box (burnt or corroded contacts). | Join D and F terminals. | If warning light goes out, clean and adjust regulator contacts. (For adjustment, see maintenance manual.) |
| 9. Warning light goes out, but battery is not properly charged. | Loose fan belt. | Check tension. | Adjust or replace fan belt. |
| | Regulator contacts corroded. | Visual inspection. | Clean and adjust. |
| | Cut-out contacts not closing, due to distortion. | Visual inspection. | Adjust. |
| | Regulator incorrectly adjusted. | | Adjust. |
| 10. Warning light gets brighter as engine revs increase. | Corrosion or break in cut-out windings or in earth connection to control box. | Check earth connection. | Repair earth connection or replace control box. |
| **Alternator systems with separate regulator unit** (Lucas 10AC and 11AC) | | | |
| 11. Ignition warning light does not come on when ignition is switched on. | Faulty bulb. | Test across battery. | Replace. |
| | Faulty ignition warning light control unit. | Test. | Replace. |
| 12. Warning light stays alight when engine is running. | Loose or broken fan belt. | Visual inspection. | Replace. |
| | Faulty alternator warning light circuit. | Check voltage at alternator AL terminal: should be 7 volts with engine running. | If 7 volts, replace warning light control unit. |
| | Faulty alternator relay. | Check for voltage (use test lamp) at all relay terminals. Three terminals should be live. | Replace relay. |
| | Faulty field circuit (worn brushes). | Check current at F+ alternator terminal. Remove F− wire and check for current at F− terminal. If no current, inspect brushes. | Replace brushes if worn. |

| Fault | Possible cause | Test | Remedy |
|---|---|---|---|
| | Faulty rotor windings. | Remove brush holder, check continuity between slip rings. | If no continuity, replace rotor. |
| | | Check for continuity between slip rings and earth. Should be none. | Replace rotor if there is earth continuity. |
| | Faulty stator windings and/or diodes. | Beyond simple testing. | Replace alternator. |

**Alternator systems with built-in regulator** (Lucas ACR and Continental models)

| Fault | Possible cause | Test | Remedy |
|---|---|---|---|
| 13. Warning light does not come on when ignition is switched on. | Faulty bulb. | Check across battery. | Replace. |
| | Break in wiring. | Remove terminal plug from alternator, and earth the brown/yellow wire. | If bulb does not light, locate and repair wiring fault. |
| | Faulty regulator unit. | Repeat previous test. | If bulb lights, replace regulator unit. |
| 14. Warning light stays fully alight when engine is running. | Faulty regulator. | Beyond simple testing. | Replace regulator unit. |
| | Worn slip-ring brushes. | Visual inspection. | Replace if worn. |
| | Faulty rotor windings. | Check for continuity and earths, as for AC alternators. | Replace rotor. |
| | Faulty rectifier or stator windings. | Beyond simple testing. | Replace alternator. |
| 15. Warning light glows when engine is running. | Faulty rectifier. | | Replace rectifier. |

# Wiring colours: Conversion table

There may be small variations in the coding system shown below, particularly in French systems. Some French systems (Simca etc.) do not use coloured traces along the cables, but have coloured dots on the terminal sleeves at the ends of the cables.

| Circuit | Lucas | French | German | Italian | Japanese | Early Ford |
|---|---|---|---|---|---|---|
| Battery or solenoid switch to ammeter, if fitted | Brown | — | Red | — | — | Yellow |
| Battery or solenoid switch to control box (dynamo) | Brown | Black/white | Red | Brown | No dynamo | Yellow |
| Battery or solenoid switch to switches (by-passing control box) | Brown | Black/blue | Red | Brown | White | — |
| Battery or solenoid switch to alternator | Brown | Black/blue | Red | Brown | White/red | — |
| Ammeter to control box (dynamo) | Brown/white | — | — | — | — | Yellow/black |
| Ammeter to switches | Brown/white | — | — | — | — | — |
| Control box to switches (dynamo) | Brown/blue | — | — | — | — | Yellow/red |
| Dynamo 'D' terminal to control box | Brown/yellow | Black/blue | Red | Red | — | Yellow/white |
| Dynamo 'F' to control box | Brown/green | Grey/green | Green | Black | — | Red/white |
| Ignition switch to coil SW or + terminal | White | Red/red with sleeve | Black | Blue | Black/red | Red |
| Ignition switch to ignition-controlled fuse | White | — | Black | Blue | Black/white | — |
| Ignition switch to petrol pump | White | — | — | — | — | — |
| Ignition switch to ignition warning light | White | Black/red | Black | Blue | Green | Blue/black |
| Ignition switch to oil light | White | Black/red | Black | Blue | Green | Blue/black |
| Ignition switch to accessory fuse | White/blue | — | — | — | — | Blue/black (indicators only) |
| Ignition switch to starter solenoid | White/red | Black (with aluminium sleeve) | Red/black | Red | Black/yellow | Black/blue |
| Ignition fuse to wiper motor | Green | Red/red | Green | Blue | Blue/red | Blue/black (no fuse) |
| Ignition fuse to flasher | Green (but white on Imp and Herald) | Grey/red | Black | Yellow/black | Green | Green |
| Ignition fuse to stop-light switch | Green | Grey/red | Black/red | Yellow/black | Green/yellow | Green |
| Ignition fuse to heater fan motor | Green | Grey/red | — | — | Blue/white | — |
| Ignition fuse to reversing-light switch | Green | — | Black | — | Red | — |
| Ignition fuse to instruments | Green | Black/red | Black | Printed circuit | Green | Blue/black (no fuse) |
| Light switch to side and tail lamps | Red | Red/maroon | — | — | Green/blue | Black/yellow to front, black to rear |
| Light switch to side and tail fuse | Red | Grey/yellow | Grey | Green | No fuses | No fuses |
| Light switch to panel-light switch | Red | Grey/yellow | Grey/red | Yellow/black | — | — |

|  |  |  |  |  |  |  |
|---|---|---|---|---|---|---|
| Panel-light switch to panel lights | Red/white | Grey/yellow | Grey/red | White | — | — |
| Side and tail fuse to N/S side and tail lamps | Red/black or red/brown | — | Grey/red | Yellow | — | — |
| Side and tail fuse to O/S side and tail lamps | Red/orange or red/brown | — | Grey/black | Brown | — | — |
| Side and tail fuse to side and tail lamps, both sides | BL: red/green Vauxhall: red/blue | — | — | — | — | — |
| Lighting switch to dipswitch | Blue | Blue | White/black | White | Red/yellow | Red |
| Dipswitch to dip beam | Blue/red | Grey/green | Yellow | Green | Red/black | Black/red |
| Light switch to main beam | Blue/white | Grey/pink | White | Grey | Red/white | Black/green |
| Wiper switch to motor (wound-field) | Black/green | Red/red | Black, black/yellow, black/purple | Blue/black, white/blue | Yellow | Red, green |
| Wiper switch to motor (permanent-magnet) | Blue/green, red/green, brown/green | Red/red | As above | As above | Blue, blue/white | — |
| Stop-light switch to stop lights | Green/purple (Ford: green/yellow) | Salmon/pink | Black/red | Red | Green/yellow | Green |
| Reversing-light switch to reversing lights | Green/brown | — | Black | — | Red | — |
| Flasher unit to indicator switch | Light-green/brown | Black/blue | Black/white, green | Blue/white | — | Yellow |
| Flasher unit to indicator warning light | Light-green/purple | Grey/blue, red | Blue | Green | — | Red/white |
| Indicator switch to N/S flashers | Green/red | Grey/violet to front, black/violet to rear | Black/white | Blue/black | Green/red | Red/green |
| Indicator switch to O/S flashers | Green/white | Yellow/maroon to front, black/maroon to rear | Black/green | Blue | Green/black | Green/red |
| Petrol gauge to tank unit | Green/black | Red/yellow, violet | Brown | Red, yellow | Yellow | Yellow/black |
| Temperature gauge to transmitter unit | Green/blue | Grey/black | Grey/red | Green | Yellow/white | White/red |
| Oil warning light to transmitter unit | White/brown | Grey/black | Blue/green | Grey | Yellow/black | Violet |
| Ignition warning light to dynamo 'D' terminal, or alternator 'IND' | Brown/yellow | Grey/black, blue | Blue | Red | White/red | Yellow/white |
| Coil to distributor | White/black | Black | Green | Black | Black | Black |
| Fuse to horn | Purple (brown if not fused) | — | Black/yellow | White | — | Yellow/green |
| Fuse to interior light | As above | Red/blue | Red | White | Red/blue | White/green |
| Fuse to clock | As above | — | Red | — | — | White/green |
| Horn push to horn | Purple/black, brown/black | Red/violet (L), red/white (R) | Brown | Yellow/black | Green | Blue/yellow |
| Horn relay to horn | Purple/yellow | — | — | — | — | — |
| Interior light to door switch | Purple/white | Black | Brown | Brown | Black/red | White/black |
| Earth | Black | Black | Brown | Brown | Black | White/black |

# Index